Computer Application in Entrepreneurship

A Guide in Operating Computer Productivity Tools in Business

Randy Joy Magno Ventayen

Computer Application in Entrepreneurship © 2017 by Randy Joy Magno Ventayen. All Rights Reserved.

All rights reserved. No part of this book may be reproduced in any form or by any electronic or mechanical means including information storage and retrieval systems, without permission in writing from the author.

Cover designed by Createspace

Randy Joy Magno Ventayen

Printed in the United States of America

First Printing: Aug 2017
Pangasinan State University

ISBN-13: 978-1985636316
ISBN-10: 198563631X

Thank you Pangasinan State University.

Sacrifice today, Satisfaction tomorrow.

—DAY CODY

Computer Application in Entrepreneurship

Overview

This book deals with the use of relevant computer programs in the different entrepreneurial activities and processes like the preparation of reports like comparative balance sheets, financial statements, merchandise inventory, payrolls, interest's computation and the like. The Objective of this lessons is to (1) Explain the importance of computer technology in the field of entrepreneurship. (2) Realize the practical application of computer programs like MS Word and MS Excel and MS PowerPoint in the different activities and processes involved in entrepreneurship. (3) Prepare business documents and reports like payrolls, income statements, merchandise inventory, etc. using appropriate computer programs. Activities of this book can be access online provided by your Instructor.

Contents

Computer Application in Entrepreneurship 1
Overview 1
Chapter 1: Introduction to Computers and Entrepreneurship 3
Chapter 2: The Internet and Cloud Computing 6
Chapter 3: The Word Processor 9
Chapter 4: Spreadsheets 51
chapter 5: Presentation 94

Chapter 1: Introduction to Computers and Entrepreneurship

OBJECTIVE: Simple introduction to Computers and Entrepreneurship and how the two correlate.

A. The Computer

A computer is a device that is used for storing or processing of data. Processing by giving the computer instructions on how to process said data.

The computer has three parts. The computer itself is composed of: Hardware which is the physical machine and Software which is the programs installed in the physical machine. The third part is called Peopleware which is the user.

A computer has many uses depending on the owner. If the owner is a videographer, they use their computer to edit videos. If the owner is a programmer, they use their computer to create programs for other people to use. If the owner is a writer or author, they use their computers to write their book pieces with the use of Office Suites which will be discussed in this book.

B. Entrepreneurship

B1. What is Entrepreneurship?

Entrepreneurship is act of setting up a new business or businesses which involve taking on financial risk for profit.

B2. 10 Basic Principles of Entrepreneurship

1. Entrepreneur Must **Be a Solutions Provider**

A business is not about profitability when a person is just starting to set it up but it is about providing a solutions or solutions to certain problems. Passion makes the thing that makes a certain business successful.

2. Entrepreneur Must **Have a Vision**

An entrepreneur is not an entrepreneur just to make a living. They must have a defined purpose to pursue. As said by Jonathan Swift "Vision is the art of seeing what is invisible to others."

3. Entrepreneur Must **Choose the Right Team**

Upon assembling a team, it is important to gather members that have the same mindset and attitude as the entrepreneur so that the group can achieve the common goal together. It is not advisable to include in the group family members and close friends especially those without any knowledge to add to the startup.

4. Entrepreneur Must **Have Viable Product or Service**

As said in number 1, entrepreneur must be a solutions provide therefore, the product that they developed must fulfill a need, be innovative and the approach must be different from that of other businesses. Also, the start-up must always give their customers room for feedback.

5. Entrepreneur Must **Have Capital**

An entrepreneur that has a good business plan always draw investors. Capital should be the least of the entrepreneur's problem. Entrepreneurship is all about solutions. When the idea or solution is great, the entrepreneur can easily get investors or a government loan.

6. Entrepreneur Must **Have Accountability**

The entrepreneur must be accountable for the success or failure of the business they have set up and not other people such as their investors or employees. It goes without saying that the entrepreneur must make sure that every transaction has some sort of record whether purchasing of supplies or the simple sale of an old office chair. The success of a business is only as good as the management of its resources.

7. The Business Must **Have Growth and Marketing**

A successful business must grow over the years. No company started at the top. Setting up and then running a business is not a one-time event but an ongoing process and therefore must be given room for growth.

8. The Entrepreneur and the Business Must **Know The Customer**

The customer base determines the life of the business. If the entrepreneur provides a solution to better the world then their customer base will increase. In business, the higher the customers, the higher the profit. The business must have a particular niche to know who its potential customers are.

9. Entrepreneur Must **Have Priorities**

As said before, the entrepreneur must have a clear goal or vision of what they want for their business and they should set priorities in pursuance of that goal. Most important thing is that the entrepreneur must not lose focus on the path on the way to that goal or vision.

10. Entrepreneur Must **Never Give Up**

This is in conjunction with having a goal and setting priorities to achieve that goal. The entrepreneur must have the attitude of never giving up. For that matter, never getting side tracked or distracted from pursuing their goal for the business.

C. Importance of Technology in Business

In today's world, technology plays a major part in the everyday lives of people. From production of everyday items such as toothbrushes and soaps to social media, with the rise of Facebook, Twitter and Instagram.
For running businesses, or designing, launching and running of a new business known as entrepreneurship, technology is a gift that needs to be taken advantage of.
In setting up a new venture, it is now easier to get hold of data that would influence the entrepreneurs if building a new venture is the right course of action or not. As for currently running businesses, processes done by hand a hundred years ago are now automated. Making the production process cost less.
Not only does technology touch production for businesses, both currently running and new ones, but also records keeping. Hence, the use of Word Processing, Spreadsheets and Presentations is a must.

Chapter 2: The Internet and Cloud Computing

OBJECTIVE: After studying this chapter, you must have a clear concept of the Internet and Cloud Computing and how they are significant to Entrepreneurship.

A. Introduction to the Internet

The internet is a global network of billions of computers and other electronic devices that would enable an individual to access a variety of information, to communicate with any person regardless of location and so much more.

When we say 'global network', we mean a network of physical cables which may include telephone wires, tv cables and fiber optic cables.

To access the variety of information, to communicate or to simply watch a video, we connect a computer to the internet which is called going online.

B. Introduction to Cloud Computing

Cloud Computing is the practice of using networks of servers hosted on the internet to store, manage and process data rather than a local server. Simple example is that data or information is not stored on the hard drive on the computer the user is currently using but by use of a website like box.com or google docs on the internet, said data is stored in a storage facility not physically located anywhere near the user. Hence, the term 'Cloud'.

Because the cloud is a remotely accessible environment, it represents an option for deployment of IT resources (computers, laptops, tablets, etc.).

C. Importance of the Internet

In this day and age, the Internet is the most powerful tool in the world because it is not just one service but a collection of many service rolled into one.

The first being that the internet is a tool for communication. Because of it, people can now communicate with the other side of the world in but a fraction of a second. Another service the internet provides is that it is a treasure trove of information. Anyone could almost every available information they would need on the web.

D. Importance of Cloud Computing

In just a few years, Cloud Computing would be important and prevalent that it would be essential for the continuation of the internet itself.

Arguments in Favor of Cloud Computing

1. **Elasticity Demand:** There are already a pool of machines or a technical structure ready for use. Cloud Computing allows the user to increase or decrease the resources of their server in mere seconds unlike a dedicated server structure which could take hours or days.
2. **Cost Savings:** Cloud Computing is essentially a better use of resources and allows the full use of hardware (memory, processor, disk space, etc.).
3. **Speed:** Speed, not just in the digital world but in the real world as well, is critical for decision making whether the decision itself is negative or positive. Everything is connected in Cloud Computing and enables for immediate interaction.

Cloud Computing basically consolidates three major needs of the century technology. These are: Autonomy with high agility and cost reduction.

E. Significance of Internet in Entrepreneurship

It is undeniable that the internet has become a vital tool for the success of businesses. Just by presenting themselves to an entire client base alone. A website must be programmed with all their information so that they can be easily accessed by said client base. In terms of:

1. **Image:** Creating and projecting the right image is very important to any business that wants to be a success. Here is where the internet comes in as it can help create the perfect, or nearly perfect, image. By having an effective website, the business can create a perfect web existence.
2. **Communication:** It is important that a business communicate and interact with their customers or client base. As it is with not just a business but with an individual as well, feedback is significant. Because of the internet, there are now platforms in which concerns can be sent to the business fast. Examples of

these are Skype, WhatsApp and Facebook Messenger. Not only that but executives, board members and owners can now set and have meetings even though they are continents apart just by the use of these platforms.
3. **Information:** The internet can provide businesses with information which they require to conduct their business by making use of web searches on web pages and databases. An electronic record can then be gathered of the said information. On the other side of the spectrum, the business can also conduct operations, which involve providing information, to other sides of the globe.

Chapter 3: The Word Processor

OBJECTIVE: This chapter will enable the user to learn what is Word Processor and most of its basic operations.

A. Introduction to Word Processor

Word Processor is part of the collection of productivity software known as Office Suite. Other productivity software includes the Spreadsheet and the Presentation software. The most commonly known Office Suite is the one produced by the company Microsoft that is named Microsoft Office which includes Microsoft Word, Microsoft Excel (For Spreadsheet) and Microsoft Powerpoint (For Presentation). Other similar Office Suites include Polaris Office and Free Office.

Word Processor is the software, among the Office Suite, used to manipulate in any way, such as formatting, the entered text from the computer's keyboard.

A1. Open Word Processor

1. With the mouse, click the start button.
    Now, depending on the operating system, how the start button looks may vary. For Windows computers it looks like in Illustration 1.

After clicking the start button, a menu appears.
2. Go to 'All Programs' and click. Another menu appears.
3. Click 'Microsoft Office'.
    Again, Microsoft Office may not be the Office Suite installed. So, as the user, you responsible for finding out what Office Suite is installed in the computer you are using.
    Illustratio
You might not see the Word Processor right away so you may have to click and drag on the scroll bar to be able to see it.
4. Click 'Microsoft Office Word'. This opens to the software's start screen. It may look something like in Illustration 2 in the next page.

5. Click 'New Blank Document'. In older versions and similar suites, it may simply say 'Blank Document'. This then opens to the software's window like in Illustration 3 in the next page.

A2. Save a Word Document

Upon creation of a document or editing of an already existing document, the user might want to preserve the changes that they have done. That can only be achieves by saving the document. With the recent versions of Word Processors, the user can save their documents on a drive or what is called a 'cloud storage' or both.

Drives

A drive is a hardware component that a desktop or laptop computer comes with and is used as their storage of large quantities or volumes of data. Computers also come with a CD or DVD drive which is used to store small quantities or volumes of data. Each drive designations are completely different from one another but follows the order of the alphabet in naming conventions.

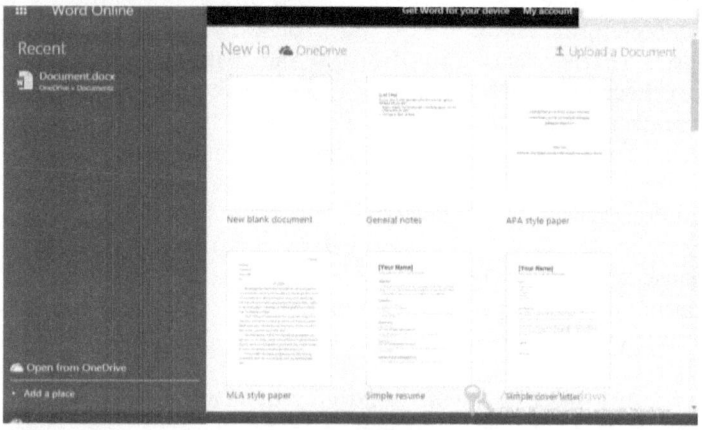

Illustration 2

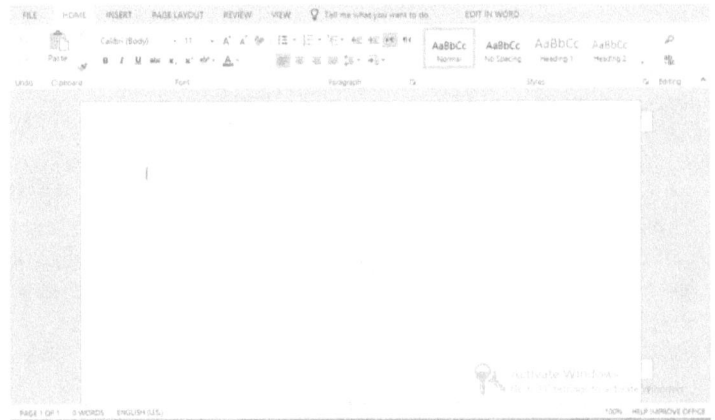

Illustration 3

Folders

Folders are used to organize different kinds of files in a user's drives. A computer comes preconfigured with Folders such as Documents, Pictures and Videos. When saving a Word file, by default the Word Processor would attempt to save it in the Documents folder. Upon what the user requires, they can change the location of the default folder. To keep things organized, creating subfolders within another folder is possible by use of the 'New Folder' button.

Save vs Save As

When saving a file, there are two options:
1. Save - The Word Processor would assign a sequential number as a file name of the newly created file until the user would assign a new file name.
2. Save As – Used when saving a previously saved file under another file name.

To proceed:
1. Click the 'Save' option and the 'Save As' dialogue box would appear.
   2a. For 'Save': User must type name they require in 'Name' Field.
   2b. For 'Save As': User must type new name they require in 'Name' Field. This will save the changes done under a new file name.
3. Click 'Save'.

File Types

A file type determines what programs can be used to access, edit and format a file and is assigned to it when saved. Default for Word Processor Microsoft Word 2013 and its subsequent versions is .docx

When a user is sharing a file with someone who has an older version of the said Word Processor, they can save the file with the file type .doc. The drawback is that features that are in the latest versions of the Word Processor that are not in the older versions would be lost or degraded. To prevent this, the user with the older Microsoft Word version can download and install a Microsoft Office compatibility pack so that they may be able to view and edit .docx files. If their Office Suite is regularly updated, they may already have the compatibility pack installed.

Another formats that can be read regardless of what Operating System or Office Suite the user has are the Portable Document Format or .pdf (Pdf), .htm (Htm) and .html (Html). Pdf is ideal for sharing but this file type cannot be edited. Htm and Html are types which would enable the user to read their files on a browser.

A3. Close a Word Document and/or Exit the Word Processor

Upon completion of work on a document and saving it, the user can close the said document and exit the Word Processor to free up space in the memory and unclutter the screen. The Word Processor can be exited whether or not the file or document the user was working on was closed. Although, exiting the Word Processor without saving would undo any changes made so it is advisable to click the Save icon first before closing the file or exiting said Word Processor.

To Close a Document without Exiting the Word Processor

1. Click the File Tab and a menu will appear at the left side of the window.
2. Click 'Close'.
   - If there are no changes made, the Word Processor, immediately closes the file.
   - If there are changes made, a dialog box appears. Proceed to Step 3.
3. Click 'Save' and then click 'Close'. Do not close the document without saving.
   - If the user clicked 'Save' but has not previously saved the file, the 'Save As' dialog box would appear. Proceed to Step 4. If the document has been saved before, its file name, type and location would remain the same except the changes would be saved.
   - If the user clicks 'Don't Save', the Word Processor closes the file without saving.
   - Clicking 'Cancel' would result in exiting the dialog box and going back to the text area.
4. The user must find or create the folder where they would want to save the file.

5. They must type the file name in the Name Field.
6. The user must choose the document type by clicking the down arrow next to the Save As button.
7. Then click 'Save' and the Word Processor would immediately save the document and closes it.

Close a Document and Exit Word

1. Just click the 'Close' button.
   - If there are no changes made, the Word Processor, immediately closes the file.
   - If there are changes made, a dialog box appears. Proceed to Step 2.
2. Click:
   - 'Save' to save the document and exit the Word Processor:
     - If the user has not previously saved their file, the 'Save As' dialog box will open. Proceed to Step 3.
     - If the user has previously saved their file, the Word Processor would immediately save the changes in the former file.
   - 'Don't Save', the Word Processor will exit without saving.
   - 'Cancel', the Word Processor would return to the text area so the user can continue editing the open document.
3. To move to or create the folder where the user would want to save the file.
4. Type the name in the File Name Field area.
5. To choose the document type, click the down arrow next to the 'Save as Type' and the user must choose the type they want.
6. Click the 'Save' button and the Word Processor immediately save the document and closes it.

Close Document and Close Word Shortcut Keys	
Description	Shortcut Keys
Close Word	Alt+F4
Close Document	Ctrl+W or Ctrl+F4

Table 1

Open a Document Shortcut Keys	
Description	Shortcut Keys
Open a document on your hard drive.	Ctrl+F12
Open a document by using Backstage view.	Ctrl+O

Table 2

A4. Open a Word Document

Before a user can do anything to a document (save, edit, etc.), they must first be able to open one.

To proceed opening a file:
1. Open the Word Processor.
2. Depending on what how long ago the file was opened:
   a. **Recent Document:** Click the name of the recent document user would want to open.
   b. **Document Not Recently Opened:** Click 'Open Other Documents' so the 'Open Screen' would appear. Click document location and browse to search for file. Upon finding it, double click name of document.
   c. **Recent Documents List:** Click the 'File' Tab so its menu will appear at the left side of the window. Click 'Open' and the 'Open' dialog box appears with the list of recent documents. Click name of document that needs to be opened.
   d. **Document in Computer's Hard Drive:** Click the 'File' Tab so its menu will appear at the left side of the window. Click 'Open' and the 'Open' dialog box appears with the list of recent documents. Click 'Computer' then file's location folder. Click then the file's name to open file.
3. Word Processor then immediately opens file.

Opening a Document in a Different Drive

When opening a document, usually, it would be located in the default drive where the Word Processor would save it. That usually is the Documents Folder which is located in the C:\ drive even though the name of the drive is not shown when opening the said folder.

Aside from the C:\ drive, the user may be able to save their file in other storage volumes such as External or Travel Drives and even Cloud Storages such as OneDrive or Box.com.

Procedures for Travel slash External Drives and the computer's Hard Drive is basically the same but when using Cloud Storages, the user must first log-in to them via browser and then only will they have access to their files.

Is It Possible To Open One More Document at the Same Time?

The answer is yes. The user must:
1. Click the 'View' Tab.
2. Click Switch Windows and a menu of documents will appear.
3. Click the name of the other document you want to open.

B. Formatting Text

Before being able to save a document and close the Word Processor, the user must actually have a document to save. This is where learning the different techniques on how to edit and format text is important.

B1. Type, Backspace and Delete

In the Word Processor, the user creates documents by typing them. Unlike a type writer, the user does not have to do anything when the text they are typing needs to go to a new line. The Word Processor continues the text on a new line for them.

Start a New Paragraph

To start a new paragraph in the document, just press 'Enter'. The Word Processor would create a space in between the two paragraphs to indicate, by default, where one ends and one begins.

To Capitalize

For capitalization at the start of the sentence or when using nouns such as names, simply hold the shift key and type the letter needed. For continuous capitalization, press the 'Caps Lock' key and type. To disable the all caps, press the 'Caps Lock' key again. For creating space between words, use the space bar.

Correcting Mistakes

Correcting mistakes is possible by deleting the letter, word or punctuation mark the user deemed a mistake and then typing their correction. Keys to use:
- Backspace Key – This deletes the character or punctuation mark left of the blinking vertical bar which is the insertion point. The user must place the insertion point where they want the deletion and then all they need to do is press this key.
- Delete Key – Select or highlight the text and then press this said key.

B2. Select Text

Next page is a table of selection methods: Table 3.

The Selection Area

The 'Selection Area' is the unmarked area along the left side of the document. When the mouse pointer turns into a right pointing arrow is when the user knows that they are in the selection area. This is the area where the user can make a selection quickly. Using the Selection Area Table next page (Table 4).

Another Way of Selecting Text

Another way of selecting text is with the use of shortcut keys in Table 5 at the next page.

B3. Insert and Overtype

While creating a new document, a user may feel the need to insert words in certain parts of it or replace certain texts with new texts. This is where Insert or Overtype is of use.

To Insert
1. Place insertion point at the location where a text needs to be inserted.
2. The user can then type the text they want to insert.

To Overtype
1. Select or highlight the text that needs to be overtyped.
2. The user can then type the new text.

A Little Tip

To toggle between Insert mode and Overtype mode, what the user needs to do is to right click the status bar and check 'Overtype' to place the Insert or Overtype button on it. Only then could they use this button to switch in between the said modes. In Insert mode, when the user types, the text is inserted. In Overtype mode, when the user types, they overtype the text. Upon testing, this tip sometimes worked, sometimes it did not.

Selection Methods	
Method	Procedure
Shift + Arrow Keys	Click where you want to begin your selection, hold down the Shift key, and press an arrow key. Use the Up-arrow key to move up, the Down-arrow key to move down, the Left-arrow key to move left, and the Right-arrow key to move right.
Click and drag with the mouse	Click where you want to begin your selection. Press and hold down the left mouse button while you drag the mouse until you have highlighted the area you want to select.
Using a touchscreen	If you are using a touchscreen, for information on how to select, refer to the operating instructions for your device.
Shift Key + Click	Click where you want to begin your selection, hold down the Shift key, and then click where you want to end your selection.
Select a word	Double-click anywhere in the word you want to select.
Select a sentence	Hold down the Ctrl key and click anywhere in the sentence you want to select.
Select a column	Before selecting a column, you must place your computer in Block Selection mode. Right-click on the status bar. A menu appears. Check Selection Mode. Block Selection will now appear on the status bar when you are in Block Selection mode. Press Ctrl+Shift+F8. You are now in block selection mode. Click and drag to where you want to and your selection. Note: Press the Esc key or press F8 to exit Block Selection mode. You can use the Block Selection method when working with columns you created by using tabs but not when working with columns you created by using tables.

Table 3

Using the Selection Area	
Selection	Procedure
Select a line	Point to the line you want to select and then click. To select additional lines, hold down the left mouse button and drag upward or downward.
Select a paragraph	Place the mouse pointer in the selection area, point to the paragraph you want to select, and then double-click.
Select the entire document	Place the mouse pointer in the selection area, hold down the Ctrl key, and click.

Table 4

Selection Shortcut Keys	
Description	Shortcut Keys
Select to end of word	Ctrl+Shift+Right-Arrow
Select to beginning of word	Ctrl+Shift+Left-Arrow
Select to end of line	Shift+End
Select to beginning of line	Shift+Home
Select to end of paragraph	Ctrl+Shift+Down-Arrow
Select to beginning of paragraph	Ctrl+Shift+Up-Arrow
Select one page down	Shift+Page Down
Select one page up	Shift+Page Up
Select to end of document	Ctrl+Shift+End
Select to beginning of document	Ctrl+Shift+Home
Select the entire document	Ctrl+A

Table 5

A Little Tip

To toggle between Insert mode and Overtype mode, what the user needs to do is to right click the status bar and check 'Overtype' to place the Insert or Overtype button on it. Only then could they use this button to switch in between the said modes. In Insert mode, when the user types, the text is inserted. In Overtype mode, when the user types, they overtype the text. Upon testing, this tip sometimes worked, sometimes it did not.

B4. Change the Font

Font is the alphabetical collection of characters that all have the same design. When beginning a new document in the Word Processor, the user is using is the default theme's font.

It is possible to change the default font by clicking the down arrow next to the 'Font Box'. All of the available fonts will appear on a list in three groups: Theme Fonts, Recently Used Fonts and All Fonts.

The names of the font groups are pretty self-explanatory. Theme Fonts are fonts which are related to themes and All Fonts are all the fonts that are preprogrammed into the Word Processor. The Recently Used Fonts are the fonts that have been recently used in documents that have been worked on and saves or have been completed.

Changing the Font

When using the Word Processor, unless the user has made changes, they are using the default theme's font. In proceeding to change the font of **only a certain or group of texts** or **all of the typed texts**:
1. The user must select the text, or group of text, they want to change. If they want to change the font of all of it, they have to click 'Select All'.
2. Click 'Home' Tab.
3. Click the down head arrow next to the Font Box in the Font Group and the gallery of fonts would appear.
4. Move the mouse pointer over the list of fonts to see the preview of the text in that font.
5. The user must then click the name of the font they choose and the Word Processor would immediately apply that font to the selected or all of the text.

To change the font **applicable for the whole document**:
Before typing any text:
1. Click 'Home' Tab.
2. Then click the down arrow next to the Font Box in the Font Group and the gallery of fonts would appear.
3. Move the mouse pointer over the list of fonts to see the preview of the text in that font.
4. The user must then click the name of the font they choose and the Word Processor would immediately apply that font to the text.

B5. Cut and Paste

With Cut and Paste, a user can use 'Cut' to remove a text or a group of and then use 'Paste' to place thee cut text anywhere in the document. In other words, Cut and Paste can be used to relocate text within the document.

To **Cut** or **Paste:**
1. The use must select the text or group of text they want to cut.
2. Click 'Home' Tab.

3. Depending on what the user intends to do:
   a. **Cut:** Then click the Cut button on the Clipboard group. The Word Processor cuts the text, or group of it, and places it on the Clipboard.
   b. **Paste:** Then click the Paste button on the Clipboard group. The Word Processor then pastes the text, or group of it, the user last cut or copied the location of the Insertion Point.

Using Shortcut Keys to Cut and Paste

Using shortcut keys to cut and paste texts or objects is certainly possible. Please refer to the Table 6 in the next page.

B6. Copy and Paste

In Word Processor, like 'Cut and Paste', a user can also copy texts and objects and paste them to another part of the document instead of deleting the text in its former location and retyping it in the new one.

Copy

1. The use must select the text or group of text they want to copy.
2. Click 'Home' Tab.
3. Then click the Copy button on the Clipboard Group. The Word Processor copies the text, or group of it, and places it on the Clipboard.

Paste

As it was in 'Cut and Paste', the procedure for pasting the text is the same

Using Shortcut Keys to Copy and Paste

Using shortcut keys to copy and paste texts or objects is certainly possible. Please refer to Table 7 on the next page.

B7. The Clipboard

Before the user cuts and/or copies then pastes texts or objects to any location within the document in the near future, the Word Processor will put the information in The Clipboard.

Using the Clipboard

1. Position Insertion Point at the location where the text needs to be inserted.
2. Click 'Home' Tab.
3. Click the down arrow head in the Clipboard Group. This will launch the Clipboard pane that will appear at the left side of the window.
4. The user must click the text or object they would want to insert in their document. The Word Processor then pastes the item where the Insertion Point is located.

B8. Change the Font Size

Perhaps the user would like to increase the size of a part of their document to stand out or decrease the size of certain texts to act as fine prints, changing the font size is certainly possible.

The F**ont Size Drop Down Menu**

1. The user must highlight the text that they would want to change the size of.
2. Click 'Home' Tab.
3. Next to the Font Size box in the Font Group, there is a down arrow head. Click that and then the user must click on the font size they require. The Word Processor immediately changes the font size.
4. Then click the text area and the highlighting disappears.

Cut and Paste Shortcut Keys	
Description	Shortcut Keys
Cut	Ctrl+X
Paste	Ctrl+V

Table 6

Copy and Paste Shortcut Keys	
Description	Shortcut Keys
Copy	Ctrl+C
Paste	Ctrl+V

Table 7

Clipboard Options	
Option	Description
Show Office Clipboard Automatically	Shows the Clipboard automatically when you copy items
Show Office Clipboard When Ctrl+C Pressed Twice	Shows the Clipboard when you hold down the Ctrl key and press C twice
Collect Without Showing Office Clipboard	Copies a selected item to the Clipboard without displaying the Clipboard pane
Show Office Clipboard Icon on Taskbar	Displays the Clipboard icon on your system taskbar
Show Status Near Taskbar When Copying	Displays on the taskbar the number of items on the Clipboard as you are copying

Table 8 Clipboard Options

The Grow Font Button

1. The user must highlight the text that they would want to change the size of.
2. Click 'Home' Tab.
3. Next to the down arrow head beside Font Size box in the Font Group, there is a button with an A and an arrow head pointing up. That is the 'Grow Font' button. Click that until the font size required is reached.
4. Then click the text area and the highlighting disappears.

The Shrink Font Button

The use of the Shrink Font button is the same as the use of the Grow Font button except that instead of clicking the Grow Font button (the button with an A and an arrow pointing up), the user click on the Shrink Font button which is located right next to the Grow Font button. On it is also an A but instead of an arrow pointing up, it has an arrow pointing down.

NOTE: Font Size Shortcut Keys Table 9 next page.

B9. Change the Font Case

The Font Case determines whether a set of characters are capitalized. It is possible to set cases according to Table 10 in the next page.

Change the Font Case

1. The user must select and highlight the text that they would want to change the case of.
2. Click 'Home' Tab.
3. The user must click the down arrow head next to the Change Case button in the Font Group which has both a capital and a small letter A. Then they must click the option they would require. The Word Processor immediately changes the case to the user's preference.
4. Then click the text area and the highlighting disappears.

Font Size Shortcut Keys	
Description	Shortcut Keys
Increase font size	Ctrl+Shift+Period(.)
Decrease font size	Ctrl+Shift+Comma(,)
Decrease font size 1 point	Ctrl+[
Increase font size 1 point	Ctrl+]
Remove formatting	Ctrl+Spacebar

Table 9

Change Font Cases	
Option	Description
Sentence Case	Word sets the first character of the first word in each sentence to uppercase and sets the remaining characters to lowercase.
Lowercase	Word sets all characters to lowercase.
Uppercase	Word sets all characters to uppercase.
Capitalize Each Word	Word sets the first character in each word to uppercase.
Toggle Case	Word sets every uppercase character to lowercase and every lowercase character to uppercase. This option is good for changing the case when you began typing without realizing you had the Caps Lock key on.

Table 10

Change Case Shortcut Keys	
Description	Shortcut Keys
Change the first character of each word to uppercase	Shift+F3 if all characters are lowercase
Change all characters to uppercase	Shift+F3 if the first character of each word is uppercase
Change all characters to lowercase	Shift+F3 if all characters are uppercase
Toggle between uppercase and lowercase	Ctrl+Shift+A
Remove formatting	Ctrl+Spacebar

Table 11

B10. Colors

In Word Processor, it is possible to change the colors of texts and objects. When opting to change the colors, the Word Processor presents the user with the gallery that has three categories: Theme Colors, Standard Colors and More Colors. These provide the overview of color options.

Theme Colors

Theme colors gives the text of the whole of the document a consistent feel. Each set of colors is associated with a particular theme. Changing the colors can change the theme of the document and vice versa which means also being able to change the color of the text or object. If the user has not changed the theme of the document at all, then they are working with the default theme.

Standard Colors

Standard colors are the set of colors which is popular or which the user or group of users almost always use. When the theme is changed, the standard colors stay the same.

More Colors

Choosing the More colors option opens the Color dialog box. The user may then be able to choose the colors they want which the Word Processor will immediately apply. When choosing to do this through the Color dialog box, upon changing the theme, the text or object colors will stay the same.

- **Standard Tab**
In the Colors dialog box, click on the 'Standard' tab to be able to select a color.
- **Custom Tab**

In the Colors dialog box, click on the 'Custom' tab to be able to select a color using the RGB or HSL model.

The RGB Model

RGB stands for Red, Green and Blue and this model uses the combinations of these three colors to create the colors a computer monitor may be able to display. Each color has a range of values from 0 to 255 and each value will enable the three colors to produce a particular color when combined. When the three colors has the value of 0, the combination will produce black.

The HSL Model

HSL stands for Hue Saturation Luminosity where, as said, each element is assigned the value of 0 to 255 but instead of paying attention to the combination of colors, what is given importance in this model is the Saturation. Saturation is how much gray is being combined to each color to produce the desired hue. Adding a saturation value of 0 adds a lot of gray in the color meanwhile adding a saturation value of 255 adds no gray at all. Lumination refers to the amount of light in a particular color. A lumination value of 0 is equal to black while a lumination value of 255 is equal to white. Adjusting the values of all three elements, Hue, Saturation and Luminosity, produces the whole spectrum of colors.

Removing Colors

1. Proceed to the 'Color' gallery.
2. Click then 'No Color'. The Word Processor will then remove the color.
   - The button for the 'Font Color' has no 'No Color' option.
   - To return the color of the text back to default, click the down arrow head next to the button for the Font Color then choose 'Automatic'.

B11. Change the Font Color

As it has been said, it is possible to change the color of the text to suit the needs of the user or whoever they intended to read their document. They can change the font color to give their document consistency or to simply give it contrast and therefore make the document much more striking to read.

Changing the Font Color to a Theme or Standard Color

1. The user must select the text they want to change. The Word Processor will highlight it.
2. Click 'Home' Tab.

3. Click the down arrow head next to the 'Font Color' button which look like an A with a line color underneath it. The color gallery will then appear.
4. The user must choose the color they want and the Word Processor would instantly change the color of the font they highlighted.
5. Then click the text area and the highlighting disappears.

Use the Colors Dialog Box: Standard Tab

Basically, procedure for this is the same except when the color gallery appears, the user must click 'More Colors' and the Color dialog box appears. Then choose the 'Standard' tab, the color the user wants and click 'Ok'.

Use the Colors Dialog Box: Custom Tab

Procedure for this is the same with the Standard Color except when the color gallery appears, the user must click 'More Colors' and the Color dialog box appears. Then choose the 'Custom' tab. Click on the down arrow head next to the 'Color Model' field and choose a color model. Type the Hue, Sat and Lum in the Red, Green and Blue field respectively. These three depends on the model the user chooses. Then click 'Ok'.

Changing Text Back to Default Color or Removing the Format

Same procedure as before except on the Color menu or gallery, click 'Automatic'. The Word Processor would immediately change the color back to the default color. TO remove all the formatting that has been done, press Ctrl+Spacebar.

B12. Highlight the Text

Same as using a highlighter to highlight an important text whenever someone is reviewing, this effect can be duplicated in the Word Processor. How to proceed:
1. Click the down arrow head next to the button with a small letter a and b with a pen and a line of color underneath it. This is the 'Text Highlight Color' button which is located at the Font Group. The highlight color gallery will then appear.
2. The user must choose the color they require and the Word Processor will immediately highlight the chosen text in that color.
3. Then click the text area.

Highlighting Text As You Go

1. Nothing must be selected.
2. Click the down arrow head next to the 'Text Highlight Color' button in the Font Group.

3. The user must click the color they require.
4. Click and drag to highlight the text. This must be done by the user as many times as they need.
5. When finished highlighting, press the Esc button.

Highlighting Text in Read Mode

Is it possible to highlight text while in read mode? Shor answer is yes.

To select a text and highlight it: 1.) Select the text. 2.) Right click the mouse and a menu will then appear. 3.) Hover the mouse pointer over 'Highlight' and the menu of colors will appear. 4.) The user will then choose the color they require. After which the Word Processor will immediately highlight the text selected.

Changing the mouse pointer into a highlighter: 1.) Nothing must be selected. 2.) Right click the mouse and a menu will then appear. 3.) Hover the mouse pointer over 'Highlight' and the menu of colors will appear. 4.) The user must click the color they require and after that they can begin highlighting. 5.) When finished highlighting, the Esc button must be clicked.

NOTE: Highlight Shortcut Keys on Table 12 next page.

B13. Applying Text Effects

When the user wants to get fancy with the texts in their document, they can apply some text effects. These Text Effects come in 16 styles and the user could create more to suit their needs. With adding outlines, the user must be able to choose the color, weight, and style of it.

How to proceed applying Text Effects:
1. The user must select the text they want to have an effect. The Word Processor immediately highlights it.
2. Select the button with a capital A in the 'Font' Group. This button is the 'Text Effect' button.
3. The user must select the effect they require and the Word Processor would immediate apply the effect on the text selected.
4. Then click the text area so the highlighting would disappear.

How to proceed applying Outline Color, Weight and Style:
1. The user must select the text they want to outline. The Word Processor immediately highlights it.
2. Select the Text Effect button in the 'Font' Group.
3. Then click 'Outline'.
4. **For Outline Color:** Select a particular color and the Word Processor will immediately outline the text with the selected color.

For Outline Weight: Hover the mouse pointer over the 'Weight' and click it.
For Outline Style: Hover the mouse pointer over 'Dashes' and choose a line style.
5. Then click the text area so the highlighting would disappear.

How to proceed applying a Shadow, Reflection or Glow:
1. The user must select the text they want to apply the effect on. The Word Processor immediately highlights it.
2. Select the Text Effect button in the 'Font' Group.
3. Then click 'Shadow', Reflection or Glow'.
4. The user must click the effect they require.

B14. Bold, Italicize and Underline

When creating a document, the user might want to emphasize particular text by bolding, italicizing or underlining it. How to proceed:
1. The user must select the text they want to apply the effect on. The Word Processor immediately highlights it.
2. Click on 'Home' Tab.
3. Click the button with: A capital B for **'Bold'**; A capital I that is slightly slanted for **'Italicize'**; And a capital U with a line underneath it for **'Underline'**.
4. Then click the text area so the highlighting would disappear.

NOTE: To remove any of these three effects, click on their respective buttons again. Shortcut Keys are at Table 13 below.

Highlight Shortcut Keys	
Description	Shortcut Keys
Change the mouse pointer to a highlighter	Alt+Ctrl+H
Remove formatting	Ctrl+Spacebar

Table 12

Bold, Italicize, and Underline Shortcut Keys	
Description	Shortcut Keys
Bold	Ctrl+B
Italic	Ctrl+I
Underline	Ctrl+U
Word underline	Ctrl+Shift+W
Double underline	Ctrl+Shift+D
Remove formatting	Ctrl+Spacebar

Table 13

C. Working with Paragraphs

It will be discussed in this chapter how to make paragraphs stand out.

C1. Change the Space Before and After Paragraphs

Spaces between paragraphs make the entire document easier to read. By default, the Word Processor Microsoft Word 2007 and above versions place a bit more spaces in between paragraphs than in between lines of texts. A number of advantages can be contributed to this including saving space and the ability to move a paragraph up or down without actually cutting or copying and then pasting it. How to do this before and/or after the paragraph:

1. The user must select the paragraphs they would want to change.
2. Click the 'Page Layout' Tab. The user would see that the current spacing would appear in the 'Spacing Before' and 'Spacing After' Fields.
3. The user must enter the amount of space they would want before the paragraph in the Space Before field and amount of space they would want after the paragraph in the Space After field. The Word Processor would immediately adjust the document.

TO BE NOTED:
- It is possible to change the space in between paragraphs with the use of the Paragraph dialog box.
- If the user does not want space in between paragraphs with the same style, the 'Don't Add Space Between Paragraphs of the Same Style' n Paragraph dialog box must be checked.
- It is possible to adjust the spaces mentioned quickly with the use of the 'Line and Spacing' button in the 'Paragraph' Group on the Home Tab.

C2. Change Line Spacing

With the use of Line Spacing, the user would be able to set the amount of space before and after each line of text. By default, the spacing for each line is set to accommodate the largest size of that font. Is it possible to adjust the spacing? Yes, it is possible by use of the 'Line and Paragraph Spacing' button in the 'Paragraph' Group in the Home Tab. Options are as follows in Table 14 at the next page.

To change Line Spacing:
1. The user must select the paragraphs they would want to change.
2. Click the 'Home' Tab.
3. Then click the 'Line and Paragraph Spacing' button in the 'Paragraph' Group in the Home Tab.
4. The user then mist choose the line spacing they require and the Word Processor instantly adjusts the group of texts.

Another way to adjust the line spacing is with the use of the dialog box launcher in the Paragraph Group on the Home Tab. By clicking this, the Paragraph dialog box opens.

Customizing the Line Spacing

In customizing the line spacing, options are as follows in Table 15 in the next page.

TAKE NOTE: Leading is the spacing in between the lines of text. It is only another term for line spacing.

C3. Align Paragraphs

The Word Processor gives the user a couple of choices in terms of document alignment. They are as follows:
- Left-aligned – Text is flush with the left margin. This is the default setting.
- Right-aligned – Same with left-aligned except that instead of the left margin, it is the right.
- Centered – Text is centered between the left and right margins.
- Justified – Text is flushed with both the left and the right margins.

How to proceed aligning the document or parts of it:
1. The user must select the paragraphs they would want to align.
2. Click the 'Home' Tab.
3. Then click either: Align Left button, Align Right button, Center button or Justify button at the Paragraph Group.

Line and Paragraph Spacing Options	
Option	Command
1.0	Single Space: Accommodate the largest font on each line plus some extra space
1.15	Set the line spacing to 115 percent of the single space size
1.5	Set the line spacing to 150 percent of the single space size
2	Double Space: Set the line spacing to 200 percent of the single space size
2.5	Set the line spacing to 250 percent of the single space size
3	Triple Space: Set the line spacing to 300 percent of the single space size
Line Spacing Options	Open the Paragraph dialog box

Table 14

Table 15

Custom Spacing		
Line Spacing Field	At Field	
At Least	Enter the minimum amount of space you want between lines in points. If larger fonts or graphics appear on a line, Word will increase the line spacing to accommodate the largest font or graphic.	
Exactly	Enter the amount of space you want between lines in points. If larger fonts or graphics appear on a line, Word will **NOT** increase the line spacing to accommodate the largest font or graphic. Text and/or graphics may overlap with the line above or below.	
Multiple	Enter a multiple of the single space amount. For example, enter 2 in the At field for double space or 3 for triple space. If larger fonts or graphics appear on a line, Word will **NOT** increase the line spacing to accommodate the largest font or graphic. Text and/or graphics may overlap with the line above or below.	

Table 16

Line Spacing Shortcut Keys	
Description	Shortcut Keys
Select the entire document	Ctrl+A
Single space	Ctrl+1
150 percent of single space	Ctrl+5
Double space	Ctrl+2

Table 17

Alignment Shortcut Keys	
Description	Shortcut Keys
Right-align	Ctrl+R
Left-align	Ctrl+L
Center	Ctrl+E
Justify	Ctrl+J

It also possible to use the Paragraph dialog box to set the paragraph alignment of the document.

C4. Indent Paragraphs

Indentation enables the user to move the paragraph away from either the left or the right margin. To do this:
1. The user place the insertion point on the paragraph or select the paragraph they would want to indent.
2. Click the 'Page Layout' Tab.
3. Then type the Left Indent amount on the 'Indent Left' field and/or Right Indent amount on the 'Indent Right field. Both of which are located in the Paragraph Group.
4. Click the text area and the Word Processor indents the selected paragraph.

NOTES TO PONDER:
- There is no quick way to double indent a paragraph. Instead, if the user has the Microsoft Word 2013 installed, use the Quote and/or the Intense Quote styles double indent.
- It is possible to indent into the margin by typing a negative value in the Indent Left or Indent right fields.

C5. Indent the First Line of the Paragraph

Essentially the same as indenting a paragraph but only the first line with the use of the 'Special' and 'By' fields in the Paragraph dialog box. To proceed:
1. The user place the insertion point on the paragraph or select the paragraph they would want to indent.
2. Click the 'Home' Tab.
3. Clock on the dialog box launcher in the Paragraph Group which will launch its dialog box.
4. The user must then choose the 'Indents and Spacing' Tab.
5. Click the down arrow head next to the Special field and choose 'First Line'.
6. Type then the amount that the user would want to indent the chosen paragraph.
7. Click 'Ok' and the Word Processor would indent the first line of the paragraph or first line of the paragraphs the user has highlighted or chosen.

In removing the first line indent or indents, follow the same procedure but instead of choosing the First Line on the list that appeared when clicking the down arrow head next to the Special field, choose 'None'.

It is possible to create a tab by clicking the Tab button on the keyboard but the only drawback to this is that when pressing this before typing any text, the Windows Processor creates the tab over and over when the user only needs the first line tabbed. Shortcut keys on Table 18 below.

C6. Align, Indent, and Space Paragraphs — Paragraph Dialog Box

To handle space before and after a paragraph or a group of it or just line spacing in general, the Paragraph dialog box that opens when clicking the dialog box launcher in the Paragraph Group will be a big help.

First Line Indent Shortcut Keys	
Description	Shortcut Keys
Create a first line indent	Ctrl+M followed by Ctrl+Shift+T
Remove a first line indent	Ctrl+Q

Table 18

- **Align Paragraph** – As the name implies, this flushes the entire paragraph to what the user requires: Right Align for flushing right; Left Align for flushing left; Center and the text centers; And Justified for flushing both at left and right margins.
- **Indent Paragraph** – This indents the paragraph left or right depending on what the user needs. This is used for large blocks of texts.
- **Hanging Indent** – This indents all of the lines of the paragraph except the first line. Used when numbering or bulleting and creating bibliographies.
- **First Line Indent** – This indicates where a paragraph begins and ends.
- **Space Before and After Paragraph** – Creating this is another way to indicate the start and the end of the paragraph.

- **Set Line Spacing** – This makes it possible to customize the space in between the lines and/or the paragraphs. Refer Table 19 at the next page for customization.

How to go about using the Paragraph dialog box:
1. The user place the insertion point on the paragraph or select the paragraph they would want to align or indent.
2. Click the 'Home' Tab or the 'Page Layout' Tab.
3. Click the dialog box launcher on the Paragraph Group so that it will open.
4. Click on the 'Indents and Spacing' Tab.
5. Depending on what the user requires:
    - To **Align Paragraphs,** choose the down arrow head next to the Alignment field and then they must click the alignment they need.
    - To **Indent Paragraphs,** type the amount in either or both the Right Indent or Left Indent field.
    - To create the **Hanging Indent,** choose the down arrow head next to the Special field and then click 'Hanging'. Only then could the user enter the amount of the indent in the 'By' field.
    - To create **the First Line Indent,** choose the down arrow head next to the Special field and then click 'First Line'. Only then could the user enter the amount of the first line indent in the 'By' field.
    - To create **Space Before and After Paragraphs**, type the amount of space (in points) before and/or after in the Before and/or After field respectively. If the user dows not want to add space in between paragraphs of the same style, check the 'Don't Add Space between Paragraphs of the Same Style' box.
    - For **Setting the Line Spacing,** choose the down arrow head next to the Line Spacing field and then they must click the line spacing option they require.
6. Click 'Ok' and the Word Processor would set the adjustment.

TO TAKE NOTE:
- Outline Level Field creates a multi-level list at least up to none levels.
- Mirror Indents are used so that there would be extra space for binding.

C7. Set Tab Stops

It is possible to set the Word Processor's Tab Stops and it is done by using the Paragraph dialog box. The default stop is where when the user presses that tab key, the Word Processor stops at the default distance. Is it possible to assign this default distance? Yes, it is possible.

Set Tab Stop Positions

The user can set the Alignment positions to set the alignment for each tab position. Tab Stop options are as follows in Table 20 above.

If the user wants to create a 'Table of Contents' or something similar, use a

Custom Spacing		
Line Spacing Field	At field	
At Least	Enter the minimum amount of space you want between lines in points. If larger fonts or graphics appear on a line. Word will increase the line spacing to accommodate the largest font or graphic.	
Exactly	Enter the amount of space you want between lines in points. If larger fonts or graphics appear on a line. Word will NOT increase the line spacing to accommodate the largest font or graphic. Text and graphics may overlap with the line above or below.	
Multiple	Enter a multiple of the single space amount. For example, enter 2 in the At field to double space or 3 to triple space. If larger fonts or graphics appear on a line, Word will NOT increase the line spacing to accommodate the largest font or graphic. Text and graphics may overlap with the line above or below.	

Table 20

Tab Stops	
Tab Stop	Purpose
Left	Left-aligns text
Center	Centers text
Right	Right-aligns text
Bar	Creates a vertical bar
Decimal	Aligns text at the decimal point

Table 19

leader.

To go ahead:
1. The user must choose the 'Home' Tab or the 'Page Layout' Tab.
2. Then they must click the dialog box launcher in the 'Paragraph' Group to open the Paragraph dialog box.
3. Click on the 'Indents and Spacing' Tab.
4. Choose then the 'Tabs' button so that the 'Tabs' dialog box opens.
5. Depending on what is needed to be done:
   - For **Default Tab Stop** Creation: a.) Enter the default tab stop position on the 'Default Tab Stop' field; b.) Click 'OK'.
   - For the Creation of **Tab Stop Positions**: a.) The user must first type the first tab stop position in the 'Tab Stop Position' field; b.) Then select the alignment in the 'Alignment' section and click 'Set'; c.) Repeat steps a and b for each tab creation; d.) Click 'OK' and the Word Processor creates the tab stop positions.
   - For **Clearing of Tab Stops**: a.) Choose the tab stop position needed to be cleared; b.) Click then the Clear button and the Word Processor immediately deletes the tab stop. Take note: To clear all the tab stops that had been set, click 'Clear All' button. d.) Click 'OK' and the Word Processor deletes the tab stops.
   - For **Creation of Leader Tab Stops**: a.) The user must type the location where they would want the tab stop in the Tab Stop field; b.) Then select the alignment in the 'Alignment' section and click 'Set'. Take note: Repeat steps a and b if necessary. c.) After that, select the type of leader in the 'Leader' section and click 'Ok'; d.) Test this out by typing the text, pressing the tab key, and typing the text again.

C8. Place Color Background behind Paragraphs

In Word Processor, besides changing the colors of the text, another way of making a paragraph stand out is to add colors behind it with the use of the 'Shading' button. Like in changing the colors of texts and objects, the Shading button has a color gallery that is divided into three categories:

- **Theme Colors** which are used throughout the document.
- **Standard Colors** which are a set of popular colors.
- **More Colors** which is a menu option that opens the Color dialog box.

Creating a Color Background for a Paragraph

1. Place the insertion point in the paragraph or select the paragraph that needs the background color.
2. Click on the 'Home' Tab.
3. Choose then the down arrow head located next to the button with a pouring pail and a line of color underneath it. This is the 'Shading' button. After which the user can choose any color they want. Or if they would want more colors, click 'More Colors' to open the color dialog box.

In **Removing the Background Color from a Paragraph**, the procedure is the same but instead of choosing the color the user would want or require, they should click 'No Color'.

C9. Place Borders around Paragraphs

Another technique to make a paragraph stand out, besides changing the color of the text or the background, is to place a border around them. Border options are as follows in Table 21 next page.

Place Borders around Paragraphs

1. The user must highlight the paragraphs that they needed to enclose in a border.
2. Click on the 'Home' Tab.
3. Choose then the down arrow head located next to the button with four panels. This is the 'Borders' button. The user then can click the border they would want and the Word Processor would immediately place the border around the chosen paragraph.

Is it possible to change the width, color and alignment of horizontal lines? Short answer is yes. This by changing the format. Specifically, the 'Format Horizontal Line' choice on the menu when right clicking the mouse.

C10. Create Custom Paragraph Border

By use of the 'Borders and Shading' dialog box or the 'Borders' Gallery, it is possible to customize the paragraph border. The following are the choices and their uses in the Borders and Shading dialog box:

- **Setting** – One click option for applying and removing borders. For application, click style required.
- **Style** – For applying border style. Scroll to see styles available and click the one required.
- **Color** – For applying border color. Click down arrow head next to Color field and click color required.
- **Width** – Enables choosing the thickness of the line. Click down arrow head next to Width field and click thickness required.
- **Preview** – Enables toggling between several buttons to apply or remove borders. Buttons are as follows:

  - **Top Border** – Click on the style, color and width then click 'Top Border' button to place the borders above chosen paragraphs.
  - **Bottom Border** – Same procedure as Top Border but click 'Bottom Border' button to apply borders below paragraphs.
  - **Left Border** – Same procedure as Top Border but click 'Left Border' button to apply borders left of paragraphs.
  - **Right Border** – Same procedure as Top Border but click 'Right Border' button to apply borders right of paragraphs.

Border Options	
Border Option	Function
Bottom Border	Places a border below a paragraph
Top Border	Places a border above a paragraph
Left Border	Places a border on the left side of the selected paragraphs
Right Border	Places a border on the right side of selected paragraphs
No Border	Removes all borders
Outside Border	Places a border on the top, bottom, left, and right of the selected paragraphs
Horizontal Line	Places a horizontal line in your document

Note: Some options are not explained here because they generally do not apply to paragraphs.

Table 21

- **Apply To** – Has two options: Text and Paragraph. Choosing one applies border around either paragraphs or texts.
- **Options** – Click this button to open the 'Borders and Shading Options' dialog box. Options are as follows:
  - **Top** – The user must type the distance they want between the text and the top border.
  - **Bottom** – Some as top but is between the text and the bottom border.
  - **Left** – Some as top but is between the text and the left border.
  - **Right** – Some as top but is between the text and the right border.

Creating the Custom Paragraph Border

1. Select the paragraphs and click the 'Home' Tab.

2. Click the down arrow head next to the Borders button in the Paragraph Group and then click Borders and Shading to open the subsequent dialog box.
3. Then click the Setting button to apply setting and Style box to select a style.
4. To select a color, click the down arrow head next to the Color field.
5. To select a width, click the down arrow head next to the Width field.
6. The user should toggle the buttons or the graphic to be able to add or remove a border.
7. Repeat steps 3 – 6 for each border to format.
8. Click the Options button to open the Borders and Shading dialog box.
9. The user should then type the distance between the paragraph and the top, bottom, left and right borders in the Top, Bottom, Left and Right fields respectively.
10. Click 'Ok' and the Word Processor closes the Borders and Shading Options dialog box and Borders and Shading dialog box then it adds the borders to the chosen paragraphs.

C11. Create a Bulleted List

A user can use the Word Processor to bullet a series of paragraphs or just any list by using the Ribbon to execute a bulleting command or by either typing an asterisk (*), a dash (-) or a greater than sign (>) then clicking the space bar. To proceed:
1. Select the text or paragraph the text to be bulleted and click the 'Home' Tab.
2. Click then the down arrow head next to the button with little blue squares and black lines, also known as the 'Bullets' Button, in the Paragraph Group.
3. The user must then select the bullet they require and the Word Processor would then add said bullets to the list.
   NOTE: Hovering the mouse pointer over bullet styles will provide the user with a preview of hoe the text would look like.

Removing Bulleting from a List

1. Select the list and choose the 'Home' Tab.
2. Click then the down arrow head next to the Bullets button in the Paragraph Group and then click 'None'. The Word Processor immediately removes the bullets from the list.

Change the List Level with the Ribbon

This is for creation or editing of multi-level lists:
1. Select list level that needed to be changes and click 'Home' Tab.
2. Click then the down arrow head next to the Bullets button in the Paragraph Group then choose the 'Change List Level'.

3. The user must select the level they want and the Word Processor immediately changes the list level.

Is it possible to remove a bullet from the bullet gallery? It is possible with the use of the down arrow head button next to the Bullets button and then clicking 'Remove'.

C12. Create a Custom Bullet Format

Besides bulleting paragraphs with what is pre-installed in the Word Processor, it is also possible to create a custom bullet format.

The Define New Bullet Dialog Box

The following are its said options:
- **Symbol** – Click to open 'Symbol' dialog box.
- **Font** – Use Font field to select font. There are fonts that are ideal as they contain many symbols.
- **Font Box** – Located below the Font field, this displays all the symbols available for one font.
- **Recently Used Symbols** – Box that shows the symbols used recently.
- **Character Code** – Programmers sometimes use Character Codes for certain symbols. If the user knows the Character Code for a symbol, all they have to do is select font from the 'Font' field, ASCII from the 'From' field and type the Character Code.
- **Subset** – Clicking this will show a certain subset.
- **Cancel** – Clicking this will close the Symbols dialog box.
- **Ok** – Click to use the highlighted symbol.
- **Picture** – Click to open the 'Picture' dialog box.
- **From a File** – The user must click the 'Browse' button to insert a picture from any location within the computer.
- **Bing Image Search** – Click this to search an image in Bing.
- **Font** – This opens the Font dialog box which enables the user to change the font, font style, size, color, effects and underline style.
- **Alignment** – This is for the selection of alignment whether left, right or center.
- **Preview** – This box provides the preview of how the bullet would look if selected.

Define a Bullet: Use a Symbol

1. Place the insertion point where the bulleted list needs to be and click on the 'Home' Tab.
2. The user must then click the down arrow head next to the 'Bullets' button in the Paragraph Group then choose 'Define New Bullet' which will open the 'Define New Bullet' dialog box.
3. Click the 'Symbol' button to open the 'Symbol' dialog box.
4. Click the down arrow head button next to the Font field to be able to select a font. The symbols of the font selected will appear in the Font box.
5. From here we can proceed a two ways:
   First:
   a. The user must click the symbol they want and then 'Ok' to close the Symbol dialog box.
   b. Click 'Ok' to close the 'Define New Bullet' dialog box.
   Second:
   a. Click the down arrow head next to the Font field then click the code type.
   b. The user must then type the Character Code in the 'Character Code' field and click 'OK'. The Word Processor then makes the selected symbol into a bullet.
   c. Click then the Font button to open the Font dialog box. The user can then select the Font options they want to apply.
   d. Click 'Ok'.
   e. Then Click the down arrow head next to the Alignment field and click the alignment required.
6. Click 'Ok'. The Word Processor then inserts the bullet in the user's document.

Define a Bullet: Use a Picture

Steps 1 and 2 are the same as in Using a Symbol.
3. Click the 'Picture' button to open the 'Picture' dialog box.
4. The user must use the Bing Image Search field or the 'Browse' button to search for images they require.
5. The use can then click the bullet they want. NOTE: The scroll bar can be used to scroll through the bullets.
6. Click then the 'Insert' button.
7. Then Click the down arrow head next to the Alignment field and click the alignment required.
8. Click 'Ok'. The Word Processor then inserts the bullet in the user's document.

C13. Create a Numbered List

Not only can a user create lists with the use of bullets but they can also create lists with the use of numbers or letters.

Numbered List Creation

1. Select text that needed to be numbered and choose 'Home' Tab.
2. Then Click the down arrow head next to the Numbering button in the Paragraph Group and then click the type of Numbering that the document requires. The Word Processor immediately adds the numbering.

NOTE: When hovering the mouse pointer over the different numbering formats, the Word Processor will provide a preview.

Remove the Numbering From a List

1. Select the list and click 'Home' Tab.
2. Then Click the down arrow head next to the Numbering button in the Paragraph Group and then click 'None'. That is when the Word Processor removes the numbers from the list.

Changing the List Level

1. Place the insertion point before the first character of the paragraph that the level needs to change.
2. The user can proceed three ways:
   a. The user must press the Tab to increase the level and/or Shift+Tab to decrease the level. The Word Processor adjusts accordingly.
   b. Choose the 'Home' Tab and then click the 'Increase Indent' button or 'Decrease Indent' button in the Paragraph Group to increase or decrease the list level respectively.
   c. Choose the 'Home' Tab and then click the down arrow head next to the 'Numbering' button in the Paragraph Group and then the 'Change List Level' so that the 'List Level' Menu will appear. From there, the user must click the list level they want.

D. Laying Out and Printing Documents

This chapter discusses printing options and essentials after the creation of a document.

D1. Change the Page Size

The Word Processor uses the paper size 8.5 or 8 1/2 inches by 11 inches by default. Depending on the kind of document the user is creating, they may want to change the size of it. To proceed with changing the paper' size (As illustrated in Illustration 4):

1. Click the 'Page Layout' Tab.
2. Choose the 'Size' button in the 'Page Setup' Group so that the gallery appears.
3. Then select the page size required and the Word Processor would immediately set up the size of the page.

Customize Page Size

Steps 1 and 2 are the same as changing the page. For step 3, click 'More Page Sizes' so the 'Page Setup' dialog box will appear. Step 4 is to click the 'Paper' Tab. For step 5, click the down arrow head next to the 'Paper Type' and then click 'Custom Size'. For steps 6 and 7, type the width and height in the 'Width' and 'Height' field respectively. Click 'Ok' in step 8 so that the Word Processor would adjust the page size accordingly. As illustrated in Illustration 5.

D2. Change the Page Orientation

There are only two page orientations, the user could use for their documents: Portrait, which sets the page lengthwise, and Landscape, which sets the page horizontal wise. The page orientation the Word Processor uses as a default is portrait. If the user wishes their document to appear in landscape, they can manually set is as such. How to proceed changing the page orientation. Illustration is Illustration 6 above.

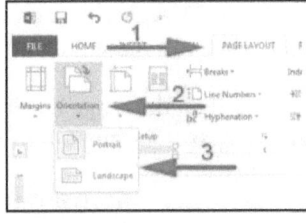

Illustration 6

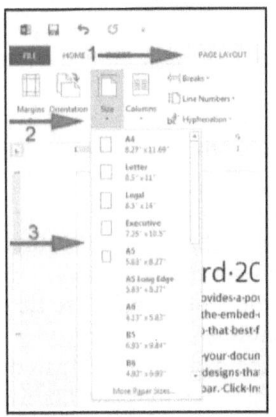 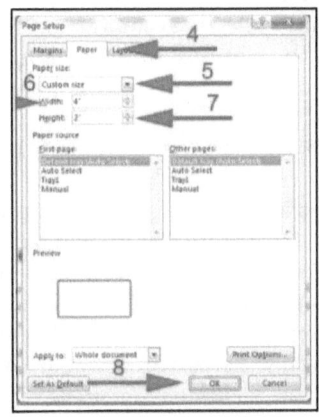

Illustration 4   Illustration 5

1. Click on the 'Page Layout' Tab.
2. Choose 'Orientation' in the 'Page Setup' Group so that the gallery will appear.
3. The user must choose the orientation they require and Word Processor then immediately sets the document.

D3. Setting Margins

Margins define the white spaces that appear on the four sides, top, bottom, left and right, of a page of the document and it has a vast effect on it. Unless said document is divided into sections in which margins affect each section.

Bound Pages

If the user intends to have the document bound after editing then that binding would take up a portion of the margin. It is possible though, to a lot a certain amount of space just for the binding. This is called the 'Gutter Margin' which is added to the 'Overall Margin'. The Gutter Margin can be added either to the left side or the top of the page.

NOTE: When printing multiple pages, it is ideal to use 'Mirror Margins' as this alternates the Left and Right Margin fields to the Inside and Outside of the document.

Setting Margins

There are only three commands the user can use to set margins in the Word Processor: 'Margins' Button on the Page Layout Tab, on the Rulers and in the 'Print Area'. How to go about setting the margins. Illustration in the next page (Illustration 7):
1. Click on the 'Page Layout' Tab.
2. Choose 'Margins' Button in the 'Page Setup' Group so that the menu will appear.
3. From here, the user can go about setting the margins a couple of ways:
   a. Using the Page Layout Tab Menu: The user must click the margin settings they want to that the Word Processor may immediately set the margins.
   b. Using the Custom Settings: The user must click the 'Custom Margins' so that the Page Setup dialog box opens. Then choose the 'Margins' Tab.
   c. In Adding 'Gutter' Margins: Steps 1 to 3 would be the same as the Custom Settings but for Step 4: The user must enter the margin sizes they require for the top, bottom, left and right fields. Step 5: They can then enter the size for the gutter margin in the 'Gutter' field and (Step 6) gutter position in the 'Gutter Position' field.
   d. In Creating 'Mirror' Margins: Steps 1 to 3 would be the same as the Custom Settings and Adding Gutter Margins but for Step 4: Click the down arrow head next to the 'Multiple Pages' field to be able to select 'Mirror Margins'. Step 5:

Enter the margins for top, bottom, inside and outside fields. Step 6: Enter the margin size in the Gutter field.
4. Click 'Ok'.

D4. Create Columns

Documents in the Word Processor have multiple columns and the 'Column' Menu lets the user choose how many columns their document would contain. Table in the page after the next page (Table 22).

For customized column formats, use the 'Columns' dialog box. Options are as follows:
- **Number of Columns:** Enter the number of columns required.
- **Line Between:** Click this if the user wants the Word Processor to place a solid line between columns.
- **Width:** Enter required width of the column.
- **Spacing:** Enter amount of space between the column that is being assigned a width and the next column.
- **Equal Column Width:** The user must click this if they want all their columns to have the same width.
- **Apply To:** Used in selecting scope of changes. Choose from 'This Point Forward', 'This Section' and 'Whole Document'.

To Create Columns

1. Choose 'Page Layout' Tab.
2. Click 'Columns' so the menu appears.
3. Click menu option required and the Word Processor adjust the document accordingly.

To Create Custom Columns

Step 1 and 2 are the same as in Creating Columns but for the succeeding steps:
3. Click 'More Columns' so the 'Column' dialog box opens.
4. Type the number of columns required.
5. Check 'Line' Box if solid line between columns is required.
6. Check 'Equal Column Width' if width of columns need to be equal. Proceed to Step 11.
7. Type width of each column in the 'Width' field if needed to be customized.
8. Type required space in between columns in 'Space' field.

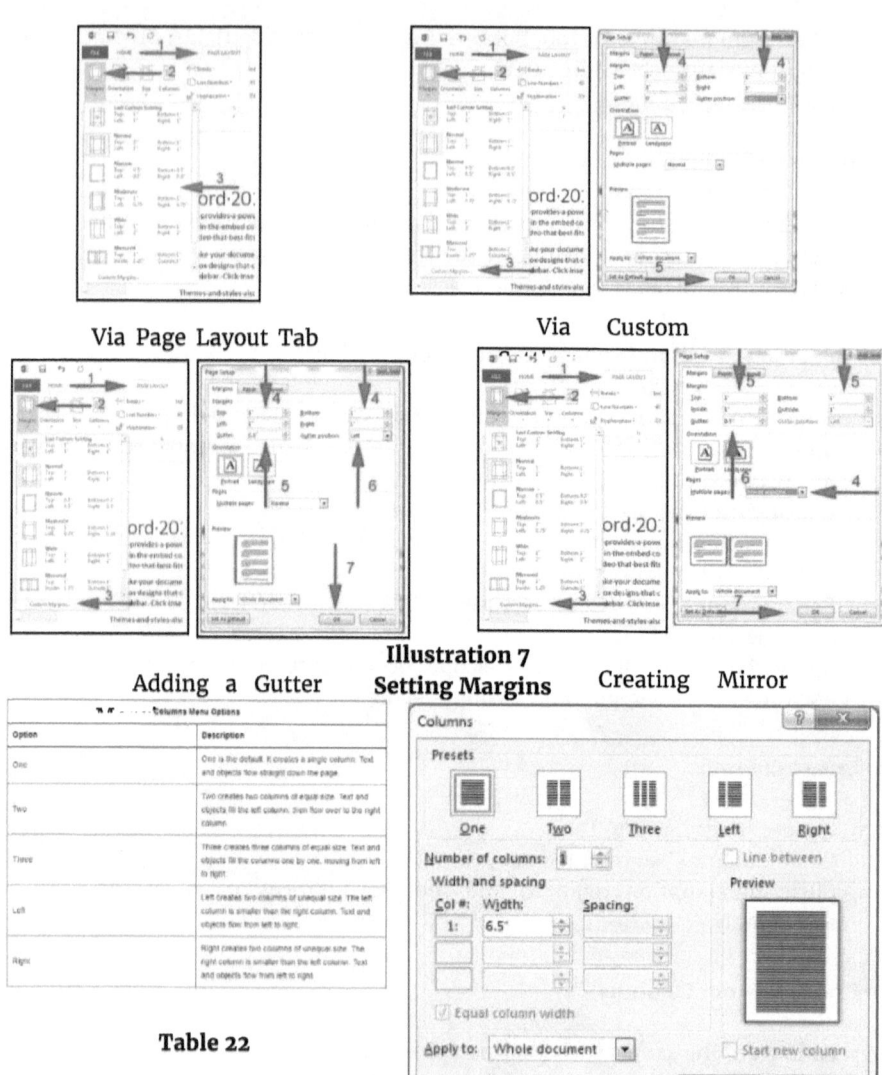

Illustration 7

Via Page Layout Tab   Via Custom

Adding a Gutter   Setting Margins   Creating Mirror

Table 22

Illustration 8

9. Repeat steps 8 and 9 for each column creation.
10. Click then the down arrow head key next to 'Apply to Field' and click the option required.
11. Click 'Ok'.

TAKE NOTE:
- Column Breaks instructs the Word Processor to begin the text that follows the column break at the top of the next column.
- Shortcut Key of inserting a column break: Ctrl+Shift+Enter

D5. Add Page Numbers

Page Numbers help the document be organized and also helps readers find information quickly.

NOTE: It is strongly advised to start page numbering on page 2 of the document.

Use Multiple Number Formats

A user may sometimes want to divide their document into different sections where they could use different formats per section. Using the 'Breaks' Button on the 'Page Layout' Tab, it is certainly possible to insert what are called 'Section Breaks'.

The Four Types of Section Breaks: Next Page, where the new section starts on the next page; **Continuous,** where the new section is started on the same page; **Even Page,** where the new section is started on the next even page; **And Odd Page,** where the new section is started on the next odd page.

Choose a Number Format

Page numbers are available in different formats. Examples are: 1,2,3; a,b,c; or i,ii,iii. To achieve the Page Number Formatting, use the Page Number Format dialog box which can also be used to specify whether said Page Number Formatting will continue on the next page.

To proceed as illustrated in Illustration 9 on the next page:
1. Click the 'Insert' Tab.
2. Choose the 'Page Number' Button in the 'Header and Footer' Group so the menu will appear.
3. The user must choose the menu option of where they want to place the page numbers and a submenu will appear.
4. In **Simply Adding Page Numbers** and **Starting Page Numbering on Page Two**, the user must choose the placement they would want for the page numbers. The Word Processor would insert the page numbers and makes the 'Header and Footer Tools' available.
5. Click on the 'Header and Footer Tools Design' Tab.
6. For **Starting Page Numbering on Page Two**, makes sure that in the 'Options' Group, 'Different First Page' is checked before clicking 'Close Header and

Footer' in the 'Close' Group. For **Adding Page Numbers**, Clicking 'Close Header and Footer' is enough. The Word Processor then inserts the page numbering.

Numbering Sections using Different Number Formats

To section a document:
1. The user must place the insertion point where they would want the new section to begin and then click the Page Tab.
2. Choose 'Breaks' in the Page Setup Group so that its menu would appear.
3. The user must click the type of section break they want so the Word Processor would insert it. The area above said section break is the first section while the area below it is the second section.

To number the first or second section:
1. Click on the first page of the first or second section and choose the 'Insert' Tab.
2. Choose the 'Page Number' button on the 'Header and Footer' group so that the menu will appear.
3. Depending on which section:
    - **First Section:** a.) Choose menu option on where to place the page numbers. This is where a submenu appears; b.) Choose the placement required for the page numbers. Word Processor inserts page numbers and makes 'Header and Footer Tools' available; c.) Click Design tab in said tools and click 'Page Number' in Header and Footer group; d.) Choose 'Format Page Numbers' so that its dialog box would open; e.) Click then the down arrow head next to the 'Number Format Field and user must click format type they require.
    - **Second Section:** a.) Chose 'Format Page Numbers' so that dialog box of said option will appear; b.) Click then the down arrow head next to the 'Number Format Field and user must click format type they require; c.) User must type the number they would want the section to start with in the 'Start At' Field.
4. Click 'Ok' and Word Processor adds or adjusts the numbering depending on which section the user is on.
5. Then click 'Close Header and Footer'.

Numbering One Section While Leaving another Section Unnumbered

Like in the topic before, the user must first section the document and then could go about numbering one section while leaving another section unnumbered.

In numbering only the second section, steps 1 to 3b of numbering the first section is basically the same but for the succeeding steps: a.) Note 'Same as Previous' on the right side of the document that is being worked on below the line that separates the body from the header or footer area; b.) Deselect 'Link to Previous' in the 'Navigation' group on the 'Header and Footer Design' Tab. This is where the 'Same as Previous' marker disappears; c.) Choose 'Page Number' in

'Header and Footer' group and then click the 'Format Page Numbers' so that its dialog box opens; d.) Click then the down arrow head next to the 'Number Format Field and user must click format type they require; e.) User must type the number they would want the page to start with in the 'Start At' Field; f.) Click 'Ok' and close all open dialog boxes and menus.

In removing the numbering in the first section: a.) Double click the header area on the first page of said section so that the 'Header and Footer Design' Tab becomes available; b.) Choose 'Page Number' in the 'Header and Footer' group and click the 'Remove Page Numbers'; c.) Choose then 'Close Header and Footer' and Word Processor numbers the second section of the document while leaving the first without numbering.

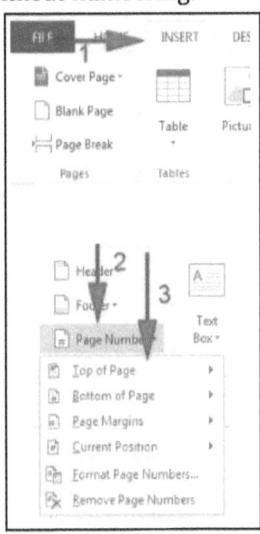 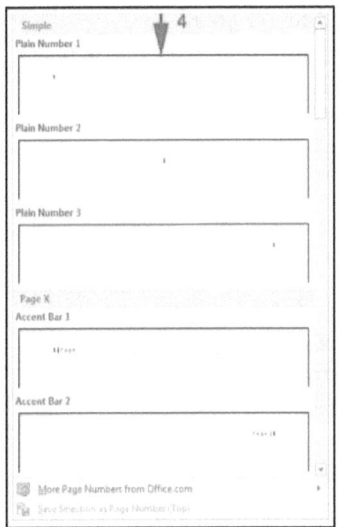 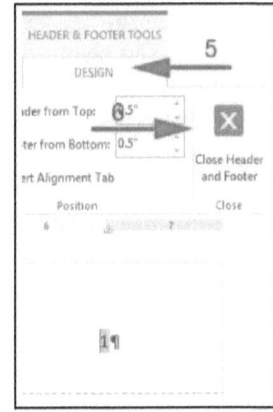

Illustration 9
Adding Page Numbers or Starting
Page Numbering on Page Two

Removing Page Numbers

1. Double click the header area so that the 'Header and Footer Tools Design' Tab will become available.
2. Choose 'Page Number' and its menu will appear.
3. Choose then 'Remove Numbers'.
4. Close the 'Header and Footer' and the Word Processor will remove the page numbers from the document.

D6. Add Headers and Footers

Within the top and bottom margins in each page is a space called 'Header' for the top margin and 'Footer' for the bottom margin.

Add a Predetermined Header or Footer

1. Choose the 'Insert' Tab.
2. Click on the 'Header' in the 'Header and Footer' group to be able to create a header. Same procedure for footer but instead of clicking Header, click 'Footer'. A menu then appears.
3. The user must click to select the format they want. Word Processor inserts the Header and Footer and makes its Tools available. On it select the 'Design' Tab to open the header and footer area.
4. Make the changes needed to be changed and when done, click 'Close Header and Footer' on the 'Header and Footer Tools Design' Tab. The Word Processor then creates the header and footer.

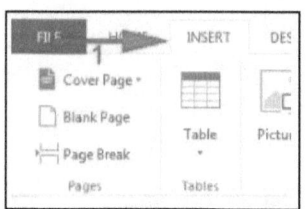
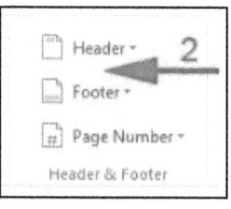
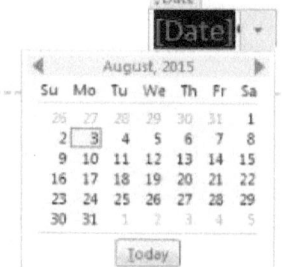

Illustration 10
Add a Predetermined Header or

Illustration 11
The Date Field

Change a Date Field

Method A:
1. Choose the 'Date' field.
2. User must type the date they require.

Method B:
1. Choose the 'Date' field and a down arrow head will appear next to it.
2. Click said down arrow head and the 'Calendar' will appear.
3. Use the arrow heads on said Calendar to change the date (month, day, year). If the user prefers today's date, click 'Today' button.

D7. Print a Document

Finally, after creating and editing a document, the user can now proceed to printing. To do this, click on the 'Print' Option on the File Menu and the preview of the document will appear on the right side of the screen. This is known as the 'Print

Preview' area. Arrow heads on the located on the bottom left corner of the Print Preview area allows the user to scroll through the pages of the document while the bar on the bottom right corner of said area allows the user to zoom in and out of the document.

Located on the left side of the screen are the following 'Print' Options:

- **Print:** This button prints the document but the user must makes sure that all other options are set.
- **Copies:** This is for when the user wants more than one copy.
- **Printer:** The Word Processor selects the printer by default and that usually would be the one printer whose driver is installed within the computer that is used. If there are multiple printer drivers installed, assuming the partner printers of these are working, then the user would be able to choose the printer they would want to use.
- **Printer Properties Link:** Located below the 'Printer' field, this is used to set the 'Printer Properties' via dialog box. Consult the printer's manual.
- **Settings:** The user would be able to choose what page or which pages to print.
  - **Print All Pages:** Prints all the pages of the document.
  - **Print Selection:** Prints portions of the document the user selected.
  - **Print Current Page:** Prints the page on the Print Preview area.
  - **Custom Print:** Prints only the pages the user specified. Type the specified pages in the 'Pages' field. To print individual pages, separate these with a comma. For example: 1, 3, 5-7.
  - **Document Info:** Prints the information of the document.
  - **List of Markup:** Print list of document changes that are tracked.
  - **Styles:** Print list of styles used in the document.
  - **AutoText Entries:** Print list of entries in the AutoText gallery.
  - **Key Assignments:** Print list of custom shortcut keys.
  - **Print Markup:** Print the document with all the monitored changes and comments.
  - **Only Print Odd Pages** or **Only Print Even Pages:** Printing only odd or even numbered pages only. Used when printing both sides of the paper when the user's printer does not support two-sided printing.
- **Sides:** Click on the down arrow head next to this field so that the user may be able to choose to print on one side or both sides of the paper with the use of the Only Print Odd or Even Pages.
- **Collation:** Click on the down arrow head next to this field so that the user may be able to choose to collate the pages of their document or not. This is mainly used when printing multiple copies of a document that has multiple pages. In choosing to collate a multipage document, the Word Processor would print page 1, 2, 3 and so on until after the last page where it would repeat as many times to print the number of copies the user has specified.

- **Orientation:** Click on the down arrow head next to this field so that the user would be able to choose between 'Portrait' or 'Landscape' Orientation for their document. In choosing Portrait, the paper would be positioned vertically while in Landscape, the paper would be positioned horizontally.
- **Page Size:** This is for choosing the size of the page. Most commonly used sizes is 'Letter' and 'Legal'. Letter, or more commonly known as the Short Coupon Bond, has the measurements 8.5 by 11 inches. For Legal, or more commonly known as the Long Coupon Bond, has the measurements 8.5 by 14 inches. Unfortunately in the Philippines, the measurement of Long Coupon Bonds in supply stores is 8.5 by 13 inches. Another commonly used paper size is A4 which measures 8.5 by 11.7 inches.
- **Define Margins:** This is for choosing the margin settings.
- **Pages per Sheet:** This option allows the user to print multiple pages on a single sheet of paper.

Set the Settings

1. Click on the down arrow head next to the:
   - **Pages:** Pages field and the user can select the option they want.
   - **Sides:** Sides field.
   - **Collate Copies:** Collate Copies field.
   - **Orientation:** Page Orientation field.
   - **Page Size:** Page Size field..
   - **Define Margins:** Define Margins field.
   - **Pages per Sheet:** Pages per sheet.
2. Select:
   - **Pages:** Custom Print. In selecting this, the user must enter the pages they want to print in the Pages field.
   - **Collate Copies:** Collated or Uncollated.
   - **Orientation:** Portrait or Landscape Orientation.
   - **Sides:** Whether the user would want to print only on one side or print on both sides of the paper.

Computer Application in Entrepreneurship

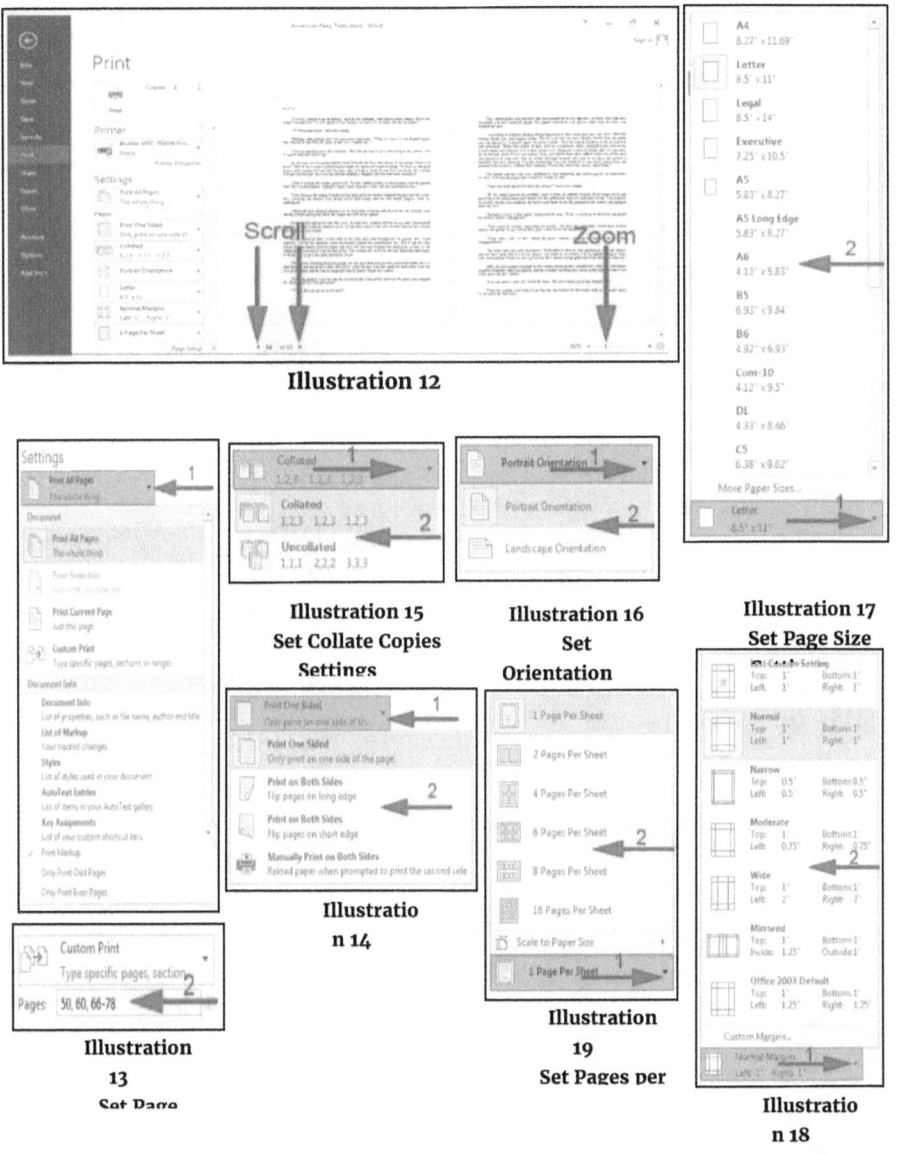

Illustration 12

Illustration 13 Set Page

Illustration 14

Illustration 15 Set Collate Copies Settings

Illustration 16 Set Orientation

Illustration 17 Set Page Size

Illustration 18 Set Define

Illustration 19 Set Pages per

- **Page Size:** A page size or manually enter a page size, not found on the menu by selecting 'Custom'.
- **Define Margins:** A margin setting.

- Pages per Sheet: The number of pages the user wants to print on each sheet of paper.

NOTE: Check Illustrations 13 to 19 on the previous page.

Print Document

As shown in Illustration 20.

1. Choose the 'File' Tab so its menu will appear on the left side of the window.
2. Click 'Print' and that will take the user to the Print Area.
3. User must type the number of copies they would require in the Copies field.
4. Click then the down arrow head next to the Printer field then the Printer option the user needs.
5. Set the Settings.
6. Click the Print button so that the Word Processor would immediately print the document.

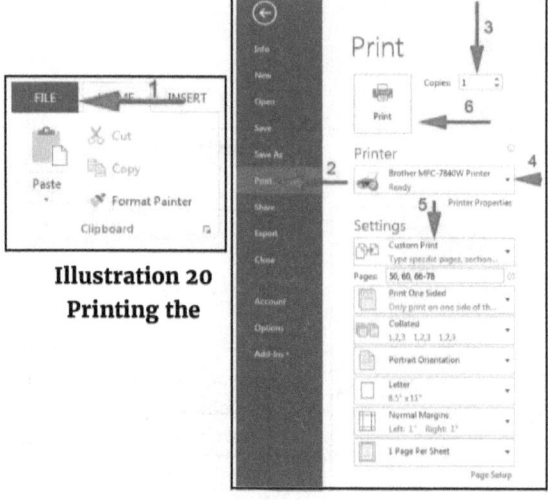

Illustration 20 Printing the

Chapter 4: Spreadsheets

OBJECTIVE: This chapter will enable the user to learn what is Spreadsheets and most of its basic operations.

A. Introduction to Spreadsheets

Spreadsheets is the second application in the Office Suit that will be discussed. Its equivalent in Microsoft Office is Microsoft Excel.

A1. The Spreadsheet Window (Illustration 21 Next Page)

When the user opens the Spreadsheet Application, they will be greeted by the following:

A. **Quick Access Toolbar**, or QAT, which is located in the upper left corner of the window provides the commands which are frequently in use. By default 'Save', 'Undo' and 'Redo' appear on it.
B. The **Title Bar** which is located at the top center of the window right of the QAT displays the title of the workbook. By default, Spreadsheets title workbooks Book1, Book2 and so on as more workbooks are opened. When saving, the user can rename the workbooks.
C. The **Help Button** which is located at the upper right corner of the window along with several other buttons opens the Spreadsheet help area where the user could search for information on how to perform tasks in the application.
D. The **Ribbon Display Options Button** which is located next to the Help Button is used to display the following commands: Auto-hide Ribbon, Show Tabs and Show Tabs and Commands.
E. The **Minimize Button** which is located to the Ribbon Display Options button is used to remove Spreadsheet from view and place the Spreadsheet icon on the taskbar. To restore Spreadsheet, simply click on the icon again.
F. The **Restore Down Button** that is located next to the Minimize Button reduces the size of the Spreadsheet window. Clicking on this while the Spreadsheet window sized is reduced turns it into the Maximize Button. The **Maximize Button** fills the screen with the Spreadsheet window. When clicking this button while the Spreadsheet window fills the careen turns it into the Restore Down Button.

G. The **Close Button** located in the far right corner of the Spreadsheet window closes the Spreadsheet. It is advisable to save the active workbook before proceeding to this.
H. The **Ribbon** enables the user to issue commands to Spreadhseet. This is located below the title bar as illustrated by Illustration 22 next page.
I. The **Formula Bar** is located just below the Ribbon optionally. This is used to enter and edit data. To **display the Formula Bar**: 1. Choose the 'View Tab'; 2. Click Formula Bar in 'Show' group. As illustrated by Illustration 23 in the next page. Illustration 24 is the sample formula bar.
J. The **Vertical and Horizontal Scroll Bars** are used so that the user may navigate the Spreadsheet window. The Vertical Scroll Bar is located at the right side of the window while the Horizontal Scroll Bar is located just above the Status Bar.
K. The **Status Bar** is located at the very bottom of the Spreadsheet window and provides information such as count of selected numbers. The user can customize this by the use of the 'Customize Status Bar' menu.
L. The **Worksheet** is located just below the Formula Bar. Each sheet contains columns and rows that the user may use to enter data. In terms of the limits of number of rows and columns, it all depends on the computer memory and the system resources of the computer used.
M. As illustrated in Illustration 25, an illustration about the Worksheet, said Worksheet is divided into **Cells**. These Cells are where the user enters their data. A cell address is a combination of a column (capital letters) and a row (numbers) coordinates. Example is the cell A5.
N. **Normal Button** formats the worksheet for easy data entry.
O. **Page Layout Button** displays the workbook is such a way that makes it easier for the user to assign printing options and to view how it would look when printed.
P. **Page Break Preview** displays the workbook in a way that shows where each page begins and ends.
Q. **Zoom Slider and Zoom** are used to zoom in and out of the workbook. Zoom Slider appears on the status bar if it is selected on the 'Status Bar' Menu.

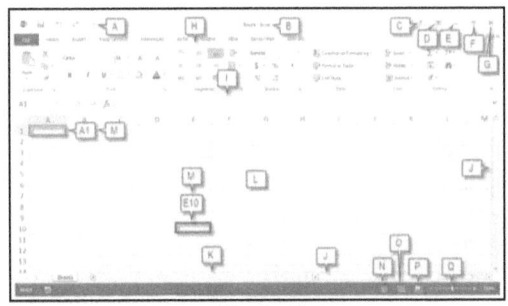

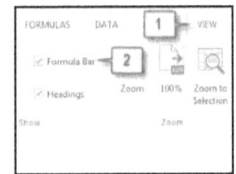

Illustration 23

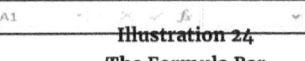

Illustration 24
The Formula Bar

Illustration 21
The Spreadsheet

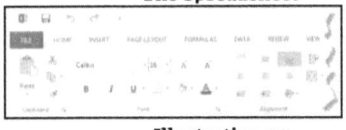

Illustration 22
The Ribbon

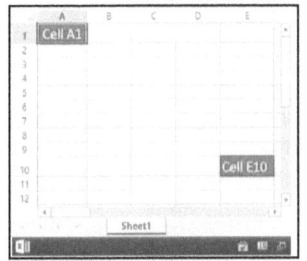

Illustration 25
The Spreadsheet

A2. Move around a Spreadsheet

Shortcut Keys	
Ctrl + Home	Moves to the beginning of the worksheet—cell A1
Ctrl + End	Moves to the farthest used cell in the worksheet
Home	Moves to the first cell in the current row
Ctrl + Page Up	Scrolls one screen to the right
Ctrl + Page Down	Scrolls one screen to the left
Ctrl + G	Opens the Go To dialog box

Table 23

As a user would work on Spreadsheet, they would need to be able to move around the current workbook they are working on. To proceed (Refer to Illustrations 26 to 30 at the next page.):

- **To Move to a Specific Cell:** Just click that cell and start typing to insert data.
- **To Move around the Worksheet One Cell at a Time:** Use the arrow keys on the keyboard.
- **To Move Up or Down One Page at a Time:** Use the 'Page Up' or 'Page Down' button on the keyboard.
- **Go To:** Click the F5 function key which is the 'Go To' key to open the 'Go To' dialog box which prompts the user for the cell they want to go to. User must type the cell address in the 'Reference' field. Press 'Ok' and the Spreadsheet will jump to that cell.

- **Name Box:** Located on the far right side of the formula bar, same as with 'Go To', it can be used to jump to a specific cell. The user only has to type the cell into it and press 'Enter'.

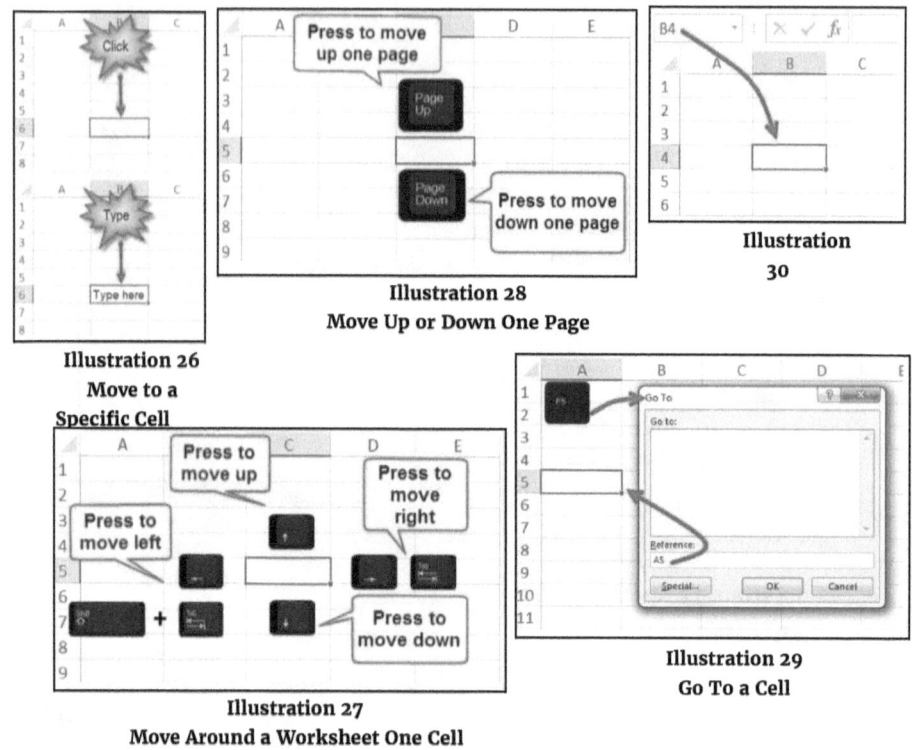

Illustration 26
Move to a Specific Cell

Illustration 28
Move Up or Down One Page

Illustration 30

Illustration 27
Move Around a Worksheet One Cell at a Time

Illustration 29
Go To a Cell

A3. Select Cells

The Spreadsheet is basically made up of intersections of rows and columns of single, editable spaces called 'Cells'. How to Select (As illustrated in Illustrations 31 to 36 next page):
- **A Single Cell:** Click the cell and the Spreadsheet will select it.
- **An Entire Worksheet:** Click the 'Select All' button located just before the column indicator of column A and the Spreadsheet select the entire worksheet.
- **Contiguous Cells: 2 Methods:**
  - **First:** 1.) Click the first cell but do not release the mouse button; 2.) Drag to the last Cell; 3.) Release the mouse button and the Spreadsheet will select all the cells between the first and last cell.
  - **Second:** 1.) Click the first cell; 2.) Hold down the Shift Key; 3.) Click the last cell.

- **Noncontiguous Cells:** 1.) Click the first cell; 2.) Hold down the Ctrl Key; 3.) Drag to the last cell; 4.) Release the mouse button but do not release the Ctrl Key. Same as selecting Contiguous Cells, the Spreadsheet selects the area; 5.) Click the first cell of the next area; 6.) Drag to the last cell like before; 7.) Release both the mouse button and the Ctrl Key. Again, the Spreadsheet selects the area. There are now two noncontiguous blocks.
- **Columns:** Click the column indicator of the first column but do not release the mouse button; 2.) Drag to the last column to be selected; 3.) Release the mouse button and the Spreadsheet selects the columns.
- **Rows:** Same as selecting columns indicated above but instead of column indicators, click the row indicators instead.

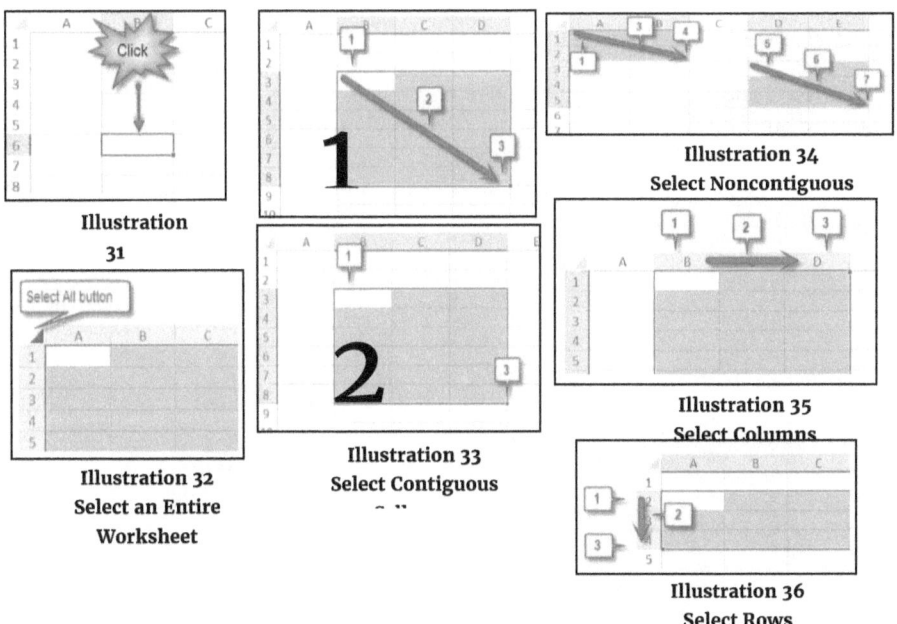

Illustration 31

Illustration 32
Select an Entire Worksheet

Illustration 33
Select Contiguous

Illustration 34
Select Noncontiguous

Illustration 35
Select Columns

Illustration 36
Select Rows

A4. Enter Data

Here it is discussed the methods on entering data in a cell. As such:
- **Type in a Cell:** 1.) Click a cell and type the data; 2.) Click the Enter Key to enter or the Cancel Key to cancel.
- **Use the Formula Bar:** 1.) Click a cell; 2.) Type the data into the Formula Bar; 3.) On the Formula Bar, click the Enter Key to enter or the Cancel Key to cancel.

NOTE: Refer to Illustrations 37 to 38 in the next page.

Data Corrections in Cells

For data corrections, use:
- **Backspace Key** – To delete one character at a time.
- **Formula/Function Bar** – Move the insertion point to where data needs correcting in a cell and use backspace to delete and then correct data.

TAKE NOTE: It is possible to specify the direction of the cursor's movements. By default, it moves down but when the user has been making entries horizontally and ends a row by going to the next row, the Spreadsheet would repeat the same pattern the next row. Otherwise the user can use the 'Excel Options' dialog box to set the movement of the cursor.

Entering Data into Several Cells at the Same Time

It is possible to enter data into several cells at the same time provided it would be of the same data. How:
1. Select the cells and type the data.
2. Press Ctrl+Enter and the Spreadsheet would enter the data in all of the cells.

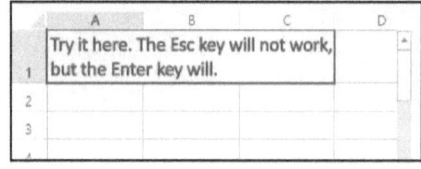

Illustration 37
Type in a Cell

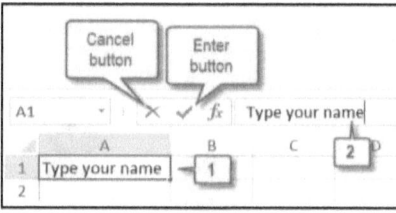

Illustration 38
Use the Formula

A5. Edit a Cell

After entering data into a cell, it can be edited. To edit (Illustrations 39 to 40 next page):
- **Edit a Cell Directly:** 1.) Double click cell to edited or moved and press F2. This places the cell in 'Edit' Mode; 2.) Use arrow keys to move up or down to where the error is located. Use the Backspace Key to erase one character at a time or just simply type the data to replace the current data in that cell; 3.) Click 'Enter' and the Spreadsheet places the user's entry in the cell.
- **Edit a Cell Using the Formula Bar:** 1.) Click cell to be edited; 2.) Click the Formula Bar so that the Spreadsheet will place the cell in Edit Mode; 3.) Use the arrow keys to move up or down to where the error is located. Use the Backspace Key to erase one character at a time or just simply type the data to replace the current data in that cell; 4.) On the Formula Bar, user must click Enter button

to enter or Cancel button to cancel and the Spreadsheet enters or cancels the data changes.

Delete Data

To delete data, two methods:
- First: Simply select the cells and click the 'Delete' Key.
- Second: 1.) Select cells; 2.) Select the Clear button in the Editing group where a menu will appear; 3.) Choose 'Clear Contents' and Spreadsheet removes the contents of the cells.

A6. Save a Spreadsheet Workbook

After creating and editing a workbook in Spreadsheet, the user might want to preserve their work.

Save vs Save As

Same as in Word Processor, when saving a workbook in Spreadsheet there are two options:
1. Save – The Spreadsheet would assign a sequential number as a workbook name of the newly created workbook until the user would assign a new file name. In Word Processor, it would be Document1, Document2 and so on while in Spreadsheet, it would be Book1, Book2 and so on.
2. Save As – Used when saving a previously saved workbook under another workbook name. Useful when the user wants to preserve changes in the workbook but also wants to preserve the original file.

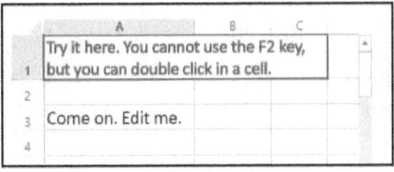

Illustration 39
Edit a Cell Directly

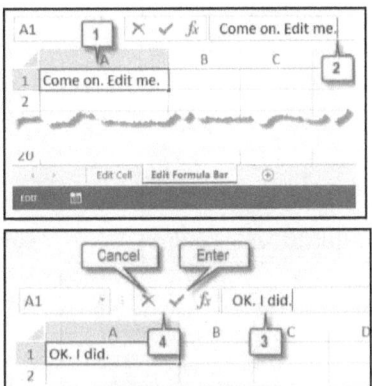

Illustration 40
Edit a Cell Using the

Basically the same with Word Processor, to Proceed:
1. . Click the 'Save' option and the 'Save As' dialogue box would appear.
2a. For 'Save': User must type name they require in 'Name' Field.
2b. For 'Save As': User must type new name they require in 'Name' Field. This will save the changes done under a new file name.
3. Click 'Save'.

File Types

The default file name used by the most used Spreadsheet program today, namely Microsoft Excel, is .xlsx which allows the user to view and edit their workbooks in Microsoft Excel 2007 and succeeding later versions.

When the user is sharing the workbook or file with someone who has an earlier version of the Excel program, it is recommended to save said file in .xls format. As referenced in Word Processor, features not supported in the earlier versions would be lost. As such, again like in Word Processor, the Microsoft Office compatibility pack must be installed so that these features might carry over to the said earlier version. Installing it would not be needed though, if the Excel program has been updating regularly.

Other file types that users won't have a problem with when sharing files: The Portable Document Format (.pdf / Pdf) which can't be edited, .htm (Htm) and .html (Hmtl) that can be read in a browser.

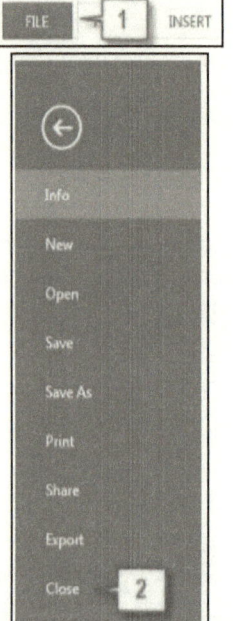
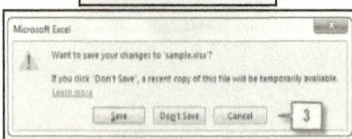

Save a Workbook to a Local Drive or Recently Used Folder

Basically, procedures for these are the same as in Word Processor but instead of saving files with the file types .doc or .docx, the user is saving files with .xls and .xlsx formats.

OneDrive

Illustration 41
Close a Workbook
without Exiting Spreadsheet

OneDrive is a way to store files or workbooks online. It is also known as storing in a cloud which basically means using an online option to for storage. Before using such storage, a user must have a OneDrive account. OneDrive is exclusively used in conjunction with the Microsoft Office Suite. Other cloud storage include: box.com, dropbox.com and Google Drive.

A7. Close a Spreadsheet Workbook and/or Exit Spreadsheet

Upon completion of work on a workbook and has since saved it, the user can now close the Spreadsheet to unclutter the screen.

Close a Workbook without Exiting Spreadsheet / and Exit Spreadsheet

To proceed:
1. **For Closing a Workbook without Exiting Spreadsheet:** Click the 'File' Tab and the Spreadsheet will move to 'Backstage' view where a menu will appear along the left side of the window.
2. For:
   - **Closing a Workbook without Exiting Spreadsheet:** If the user has not made any changes since they last edited to workbook, the Spreadsheet closes the workbook immediately.
   - **Closing a Workbook and Exiting Spreadsheet:** If the user has not made any changes since they last edited to workbook, the Spreadsheet closes immediately.
   - If the user has made changes to the workbook or of the user has never save the workbook, a prompt will appear and the user will be able to proceed to step 3.
3. Click 'Save' to save the workbook and 'Close' or 'Cancel' to stop Close operation. It is highly recommended to save the workbook first before closing the Spreadsheet program.
   - If the workbook is newly created, the 'Save As' dialog box opens. Proceed to step 4.
   - If the workbook has been previously saved, Spreadsheet will save the file in the same location it was before using the same file name and type it already had.
   - If the user has clicked 'Don't Save', the Spreadsheet closes the workbook without saving.
   - If the user has clicked 'Cancel', the Spreadsheet returns to the workbook and they can continue editing.
4. The user must find or create the folder where they would want to save the workbook.
5. Type the name of the workbook in the 'File Name' field.

6. The user must click the down arrow head next to the 'Save as Type' field and then they should click the workbook type they would require.
7. Click 'Save' and the Spreadsheet saves the workbook and closes the file.

Close Workbook and Close Excel Shortcut Keys

Description	Shortcut Keys
Close Excel	Alt+F4
Close Workbook	Ctrl + W or Ctrl + F4

Table 24

- Negation (-10)
- Percent (%)
- Power (^)
- Multiplication and division
- Addition and subtraction
- Joining text (&)
- Comparison (= < > <= >= <>)

Illustration 42

Mathematical Operators

Symbol	Calculation Type	Formula	Result
+	Addition	=1+1	2
-	Subtraction	=4-3	1
-	Negation	=-1	-1
*	Multiplication	=2*3	6
/	Division	=6/2	3
^	Exponential (Raises to a power)	=3^2	9
%	Percent	=10%	10%

Table 25

B. Formulas

The cornerstone of Spreadsheet use is its ability to perform calculations. Hence, the use of formulas.

B1. Create a Spreadsheet Formula

Spreadsheet has the ability to perform mathematical equations such as addition and subtraction by use of formulas. The user must type the formula where they want the result to appear and it must start with the equal sign. Table 25 lists all of the mathematical operators used in Spreadsheet.

In referencing a cell, the user must use the cell address in the formula. If a cell contains a numbers, like say B4 contains the value 45.678 and the formula in C4 is =B4+55, the Spreadsheet will use the number value in the formula, thus C4's value will be the value of B4 which is 45.678 plus 55. If the cell contains a text value though, the formula would return and error. For example, cell B4 contains the word 'right' and, as said the formula in C4 is =B4+55, the result would be an error.

When creating formulas please be mindful of precedence or the order in which Spreadsheet does calculations. Said program uses the following order in Illustration 42. Examples in Illustration 43 at the next page contains valid formulas.

B2. Use Spreadsheet Functions

Functions enable the user to make useful calculations. The most well-known Spreadsheet program, namely Microsoft Excel, has over 300 functions that the user can use. They can either be used alone or as part of a larger formula.

Reference Operators

Reference Operators refer to a cell or a group of cell and there are three types:
- **Range** is that that refers to the cells between and including the reference or references A Range Reference includes the two reference cell addresses separated by a colon. I.e., **A1:A3 or C1:E3**. A Spreadsheet workbook has multiple sheets but it is possible to reference these as well by typing the name of the sheet after the equal sign followed by an exclamation point and then the cell reference. If the sheet name has a space, simply enclose the sheet name in single quotes. Refer to Illustration 44.
- **Union** refers to two or more references that are separated by a comma. Basically, these contain two more numbers, Range References, cell addresses or functions. For example, in the Union Reference of **A3,B4:B6,C5**. Refer to Illustration 45.
- **Intersection** Reference refers to all the cells that two or more Range References or operators have in common. As said before, an Intersection Reference consists of two Range Reference separated by a space. E.g. **A1:C3 C1:E3** refers to the cells **C1:C3** as the intersection. Refer to Illustration 46.

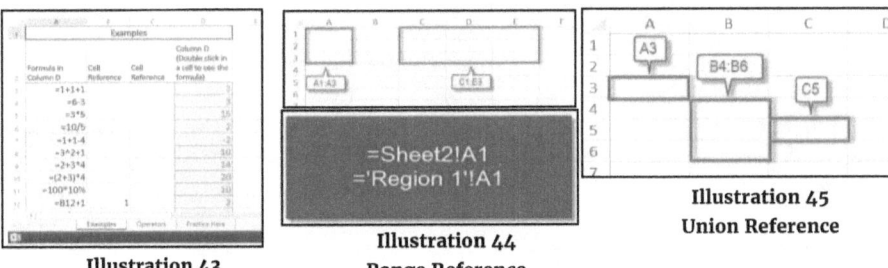

Illustration 43

Illustration 44
Range Reference

Illustration 45
Union Reference

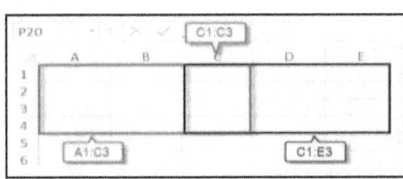

Illustration 46
Intersection

Functions

These are prewritten formulas that differ from regular formulas because the user supplies the value but not the operators. An example would be the SUM Function to add numbers. In using functions:

- If function starts the formula, it needs to be preceded with an equal sign.
- Function name needs to be specified.
- Enclose Arguments, or the values, with parenthesis. With the Sum Function, Arguments can be either number values and/or cell address which contain numbered values.
- To separate arguments, use commas.

Illustration 47

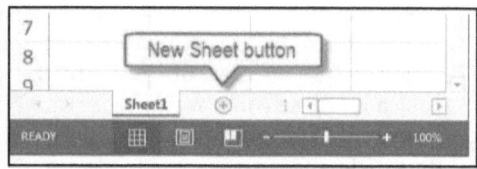

Illustration 48
Create a New Worksheet

In the example function as illustrated in Illustration 47 on the previous page:
- An equal sign starts the formula.
- The name of the function is SUM.
- The arguments are 2, 13, A1, B2:C7.
- Commas separate the arguments while they are enclosed in a parenthesis.

When entering a function name, after the first letter, the AutoComplete list appears. A user can click the function they require from the list to complete the entry quickly.

Create/Rename a Worksheet

In creating a new worksheet, the user must click the new sheet button which is located next to the last worksheet tab and just before the horizontal scroll bar. Refer to Illustration 47 on the previous page.

For renaming a worksheet, the user must right click on the worksheet name on the tab. A menu will appear and the user must choose rename. The user can then proceed renaming the worksheet.

B3. Use Spreadsheet Formulas to Comparisons or Joint Text

In addition to formulas, users can use comparison operators to make comparisons. Comparison operators used in Spreadsheet are as follows (Table 26):

Comparison Operators

Operator	Name	Description	Example	Result
=	Equal	Determines if one value is equal to another value	=1=1	TRUE
<>	Not equal	Determines if one value is not equal to another value	=1<>1	FALSE
>	Greater than	Determines if one value is greater than another value	=1>2	FALSE
<	Less than	Determines if one value is less than another value	=1<2	TRUE
>=	Greater than equal to	Determines if one value is greater than or equal to another value	=1>=2	FALSE
<=	Less than equal to	Determines if one value is less than or equal to another value	=3<=2	FALSE

Table 26

The values TRUE and FALSE are logical values which can only be one of the two options. In calculations, TRUE is equal to 1 while FALSE is equal to 0.

Joining Text

Joining texts is called the process of Concatenation and makes use of the Concatenation operator (&).

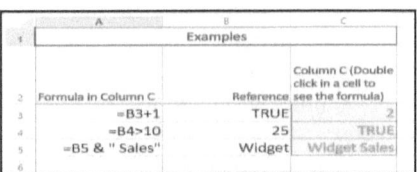

Illustration 49
Joining Text Examples

Observe from Illustration 49 that when including text in a formula, the user must enclose text in Double Quotes.

B4. Name Cells, Cell Ranges and Constants

It is possible to name cells, cell ranges and constants in Spreadsheet and are easier to remember when creating formulas. The 'Range' dialog box should be used to rename cells and cell ranges. Naming conventions or rules are as follows:
- Must be lesser than 255 characters.
- Must start with a letter or backslash.
- Symbols cannot be included except:
- Dot and/or underscore which are used as separator.

The name for a cell, cell range or constant can be recognizable to only one worksheet or the entire workbook. E.g. User names cell A1 on Sheet1 and sets the scope to the same sheet. Now, he can't use that set name in Sheet2 because the scope set for that name is only in Sheet1. The user can, however, repeat the same process only instead of Sheet1, said process will be done in Sheet2. Setting the scope of the name is not limited to 1 worksheet as the user can set the scope of said name to the entire workbook. That way when cell A1 is named, it can be used to create formulas in whatever sheet in the workbook.

Name a Cell or Range of Cells (As seen in Illustration 50 next page.) or **Several Ranges at Once** (Refer to Illustration 51 next page.)

1. For:
   - **Cell or Range of Cells:** User must select cell or cell range they want to name.
   - **Several Ranges at Once:** User must select the range they want to name and include labels.
2. Click 'Formulas' Tab.
3. For:
   - **Cell or Range of Cells:** Choose 'Define Name' so that the 'New Name' dialog box appears.
   - **Several Ranges at Once:** Choose 'Create from Selection' in the 'Defined Names' group which opens the 'Create Names from Selection' dialog box.
4. For:
   - **Cell or Range of Cells:** User must type the name they want to give the cell or range in the Name field.
   - **Several Ranges at Once:** Choose the location of the Range Names.
5. For:
   - **Cell or Range of Cells:** Click the down arrow head next to the 'Scope' field then select scope of the name.
   - **Several Ranges at Once:** Click 'Ok' and the Spreadsheets name the ranges where they appear in the name box.
6. Only for **Naming a Cell or Range of Cells:** The user can finally click 'Ok' and Spreadsheet creates the named cell or range where said name appears on the name box.

The Spreadsheet can name several ranges once by using the 'Selection' option. To be able to edit or delete a Name Range, the user must use the Name Manager on the Formulas Tab.

Delete or **Edit a Named Range** or **Create a Named Constant** (Refer to Illustrations 52-54 the next page)

1. Click on the Formulas Tab.
2. For:
   - **Delete or Edit a Named Range:** Choose 'Name Manager' in the 'Defined Names' group so that the 'Name Manager' dialog box opens.
   - **Creating a Named Constant:** Choose 'Define Name' and the New Name dialog box would open.

Computer Application in Entrepreneurship

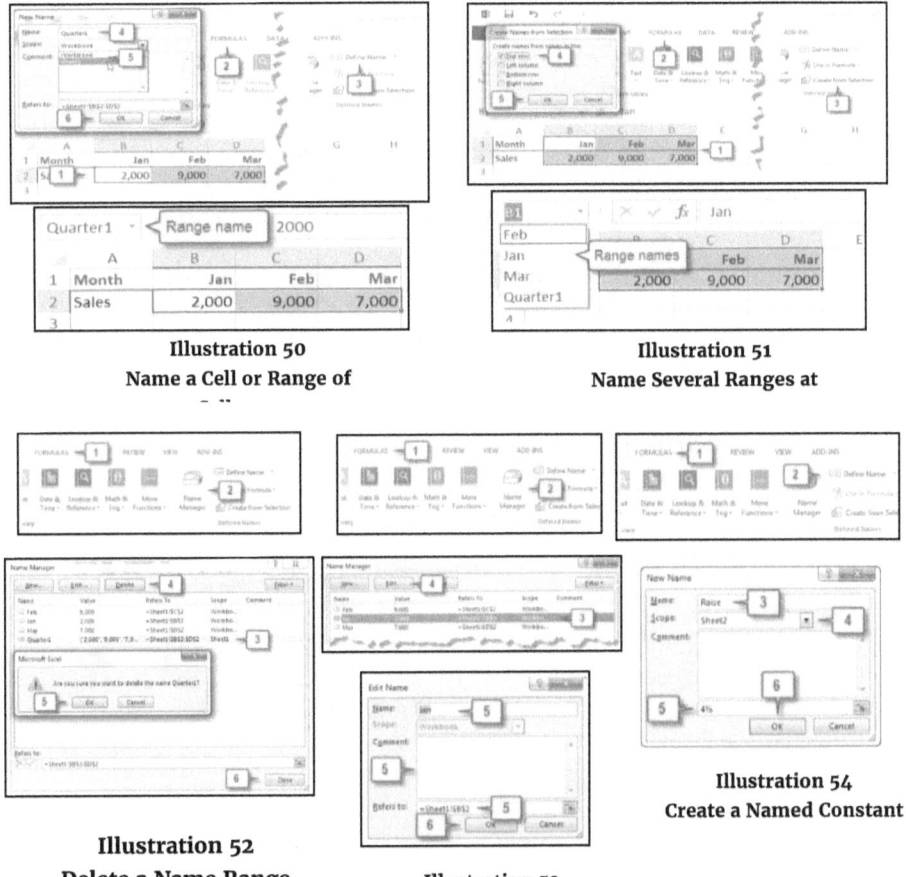

Illustration 50
Name a Cell or Range of

Illustration 51
Name Several Ranges at

Illustration 52
Delete a Name Range

Illustration 53
Edit a Name Range

Illustration 54
Create a Named Constant

3. For:
   - **Delete or Edit a Named Ranger:** User must click the range they want to delete or edit by holding down the Ctrl Key and then selecting multiple ranges.
   - **Creating a Named Constant:** User must type the name they would want the constant to have on the Name field.
4. For:
   - **Delete:** User can then click Delete but Spreadsheet will ask "Are you sure you want to delete...?".
   - **Edit:** User can now click Edit. The Edit Name dialog box then appears.
   - **Creating a Named Constant:** User must click the down arrow head next to the Scope field and then they can choose the scope they require.
5. For:

65

- **Delete:** Click Ok and the Spreadsheet deletes the range name.
- **Edit:** User can now make the changes.
- **Creating a Named Constant:** User must type the value they want to assign the constant in the 'Refers to' field.

6. For:
   - **Delete:** The user can then click Close so that the Spreadsheet closes the Name Manager dialog box.
   - **Edit:** Click Ok so that the Spreadsheet returns to the Name Manager dialog box.
   - **Creating a Named Constant:** Click Ok so that the Spreadsheet may be able to name the constant.
7. For **Edit**, repeat steps three to six for editing additional ranges or the user can click Close when they are finished.

Examples of Formulas that Uses Names

=January+February+March   =Quarter_1+QQuarter_2   =January*10%

B5. Enter Formulas

In Spreadsheets, formulas are used to do mathematical equations, comparisons and join text. Formulas can be entered by typing them directly to the cell or into the Formula bar. If the Formula bar cannot be seen: 1.) Click View Tab; 2.) Check the 'Formula Bar' Option in the 'Show' group and this is only where Spreadsheet will be able to display the Formula Bar.

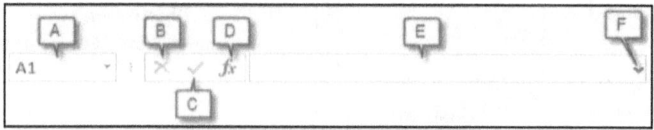

Illustration 55 The Formula Bar

A. The **Name Box** displays the cell address or name of the current cell. To see the other range names, click the down arrow head next of this. To move to a certain cell or cell range, click their names.

B. The **Cancel Button** is used when canceling the newly entered data or the changes done.
C. The **Enter Button** is clicked to enter data or changes.
D. The **Insert Function** Button is clicked when to open the 'Insert Function' dialog box.
E. The **Formula bar** is where the user enters formulas and other data.
F. The **Chevron** is clicked to enlarge the Formula Bar.

Type a Formula, Click and Drag to Select Cells and Cell Ranges, Click to Select another Sheet and **Click to Select a Range of Sheets**

1. User must click the cell where they want the result of the formula to appear.
2. For:
   - **Typing a Formula:** Type the formula in the cell or in the Formula Bar.
   - **Click and Drag to Select Cells and Cell Ranges:** Begin typing the formula in the cell or in the Formula Bar. When the user wants to reference a cell, they have to click it. Then continue typing. When the user wants to reference a range, they must click and drag to select the range. Then continue typing again.
   - **Click to Select another Sheet:** Begin typing the formula in the cell or in the Formula Bar. When the user want to reference another sheet, they must click the sheet.
   - **Click to Select a Range of Sheets:** Begin typing the formula.
3. For:
   - **Typing a Formula and Click** and **Drag to Select Cells and Cell Ranges:** User must click the enter button on the Formula Bar when they have completed the formula. Spreadsheet will calculate and display the result in the cell chosen when the user has typed said formula.
   - **Click to Select another Sheet:** User must click the cell or click and drag the cell range they want to reference.
   - **Click to Select a Range of Sheets:** Click the first sheet of the workbook.
4. For:
   - **Click to Select another Sheet:** Continue typing the formula.
   - **Click to Select a Range of Sheets:** Press the Shift Key then the last sheet of the workbook.
5. For:
   - **Click to Select another Sheet:** Click the Enter button on the Formula Bar when the formula is completed.
   - **Click to Select a Range of Sheets:** User must select the tools they want to include.
6. For **Clicking to Select a Range of Sheets**, click the Enter button on the Formula Bar when the formula is completed.

B6. Use the Function Wizard

The Function Wizard can help the user greatly by providing the function they want and providing them with a step-by-step guide on how to use it. To access it, click 'Insert Function' on the Formula Bar or Insert Function button on the Formulas Tab.

On the dialog box that opens, user must search for the function they require either by typing it on the 'Search for Function' fields or on the list below said field.

Each function has its own dialog box which is called the 'Function Specific' dialog box.

To proceed (Refer to Illustration 56 next page):
1. User must move to the cell where they want the result of the formula to appear.
2. Begin typing in the cell through the Formula Bar.
3. When the user need to use a function, they must type the function name.
4. Upon seeing the function name on the AutoComplete list, user must click it.
5. User must click the 'Insert Function' button so the dialog box for the selected function opens.
6. Enter the arguments the user needs to use.
7. When function is completed, click 'Ok'.
8. Continue entering the formula.
9. Click the Enter button on the Formula Bar when the formula is completed.

B7. Create an Array Formula

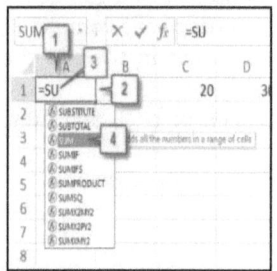

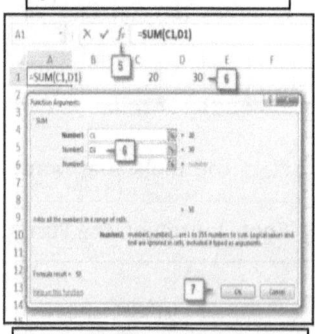

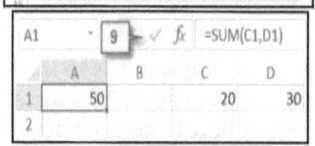

Illustration

- Insert a cell within the array.

Array Formulas enable the user to make a lot of calculations with only a single formula. There are two type pf these:

a. **Multi-cell** which performs multiple calculations that also returns multiple results. (Example is Illustration 57.)

b. **Single Cell** which, like multi-cell, performs multiple calculations but returns only a single result.

Enter a Multi-cell Array Formula (Refer to Illustration 58 next page.)

1. User must select cells where they want the results to appear.
2. The user can then type the formula.
3. Press down Ctrl+Shift+Enter and the Spreadsheet calculates the results, places them in the selected cells.

As said before, with a multi-cell array, several cells share the same formula. As a result, the user cannot:
- Change the contents of any of the cells.
- Clear, move, or delete any of the cells.

If any of these have been done, an error message would be returned.

As we have said before, starting a Single Cell formula by selecting one cell. Like with a Multi-cell formula, the users can end the typing by pressing Ctrl+Shift+Enter. Also like a Multi-cell formula, a Single Cell formula will perform multiple calculations but would only return a single result. Take for example Illustration 59.

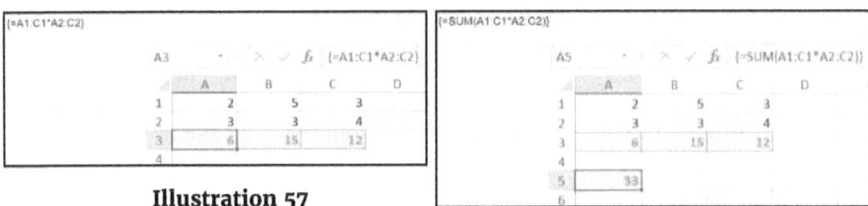

Illustration 57

Illustration 57 and 59 Example Explanations

Illustration 59

Illustration 57

The formula multiplies the values located in Row 1 Columns A, B and C with the values located in Row 2 Columns A, B and C and places the results in Row 3 Columns A, B and C.

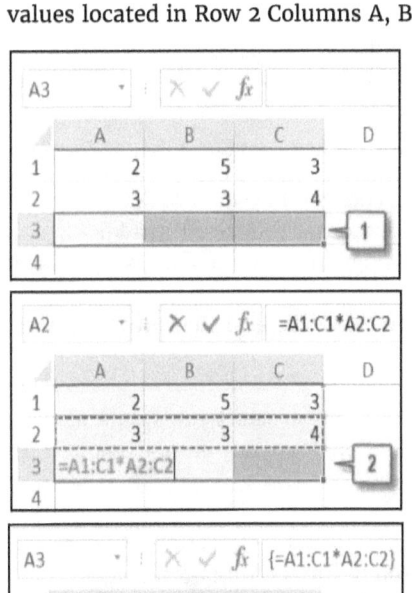

Illustration 59

The formula adds together the results of the calculations in Illustration 57 and returns the result in a single cell.

Enter a Single Cell Array Formula

1. User must select cell where they want the result to appear.
2. They can then type the formula.
3. Press then the Ctrl+Shift+Enter and the Spreadsheet will calculate the result and put that result in the cell the user selected.

Enter an Array Formula

Method A:

1. User can click anywhere in the cell range that contains the formula.
2. The user can use the Formula Bar to edit.

Method B:
1. User must first click the range that contains the formula.
2. Click on the Home Tab.
3. Choose the 'Find and Select' in the 'Editing' group and a menu will open.
4. Click on 'Go To' and its dialog box will appear.
5. User must click the 'Special' button.
6. User can then click 'Current Array'.
7. Click 'Ok' and this is where the user can now use the Formula Bar to edit.

Illustration 58

C. Popular Functions

Here, Spreadsheet Popular Functions will be introduced.

C1. Use AutoSum

AutoSum has features that will help the user calculate SUM, COUNT, AVERAGE, MIN or MAX quickly through Spreadsheet.
AutoSum a Column or Row, a Range of Columns, a Range of Rows, a Range (In General), Both Columns and Rows, the Grand Total

1. For:
   - Column: User must click the cell under the column they want to add.
   - Row: User must click the cell to the right of the row they want to add.
   - Range of Columns: User must select the range under the columns they want to add.
   - Range of Rows: User must select the range to the right of the rows they want to add.
   - Range: User must select the range.
   - Both Columns and Rows, Grand Total: User must select the range of cells including an empty column to the right of the last not empty one and an empty row after the last not empty one.
2. Then they must click the Home Tab.
3. For:
   - Column: Just click then the AutoSum button in the 'Editing' group.
   - Row: Click then the AutoSum button in the 'Editing' group. Spreadsheet enters the SUM Function and selects the cells to add. The user can edit the selection of cells.

- Range of Columns, Range of Rows, Range (In General), Both Columns and Rows, Grand Total: Proceed to step 4.
4. User can now press Enter and the Spreadsheet will use the SUM Function to add the column, row or a range of both, or just the clicked range by the user, or both column and rows and finally, the grand total.

NOTE: Refer to Illustrations 60 to 65 in the next page and Illustration 66 in the page after that..

C2. Use the SUM Function

As its name implies, the SUM Function of Spreadsheet adds values which can include up to 255 arguments.
Syntax: SUM(argument1, argument2, ...)
When using said function, the treatment of data type by Spreadsheet may depend on whether it is located in a cell, an array, or an argument.
When a cell contains a logical values (TRUE or FALSE), text or an error value, Spreadsheet ignores the cell but if an array contains the said values, Spreadsheet ignores the logical values, text or error value.

C3. Use the COUNT Function

What he COUNT Function does is that it counts the number of numbers in the work sheet which, like the SUM Function, could include up to 255 arguments.
Syntax: COUNT(argument1, argument2, ...) The first argument is required, the ones that follow are optional.
Upon using the function, how Spreadsheet may treat the data depends on whether the data type is located in a cell, in an array or in an argument. With this, TRUE and False are logical values and dates are stored as numbers. By default, Spreadsheet considers numbers preceded by an apostrophe text but when using a formula or a function, Spreadsheet considers numbers enclosed in double quotes text.

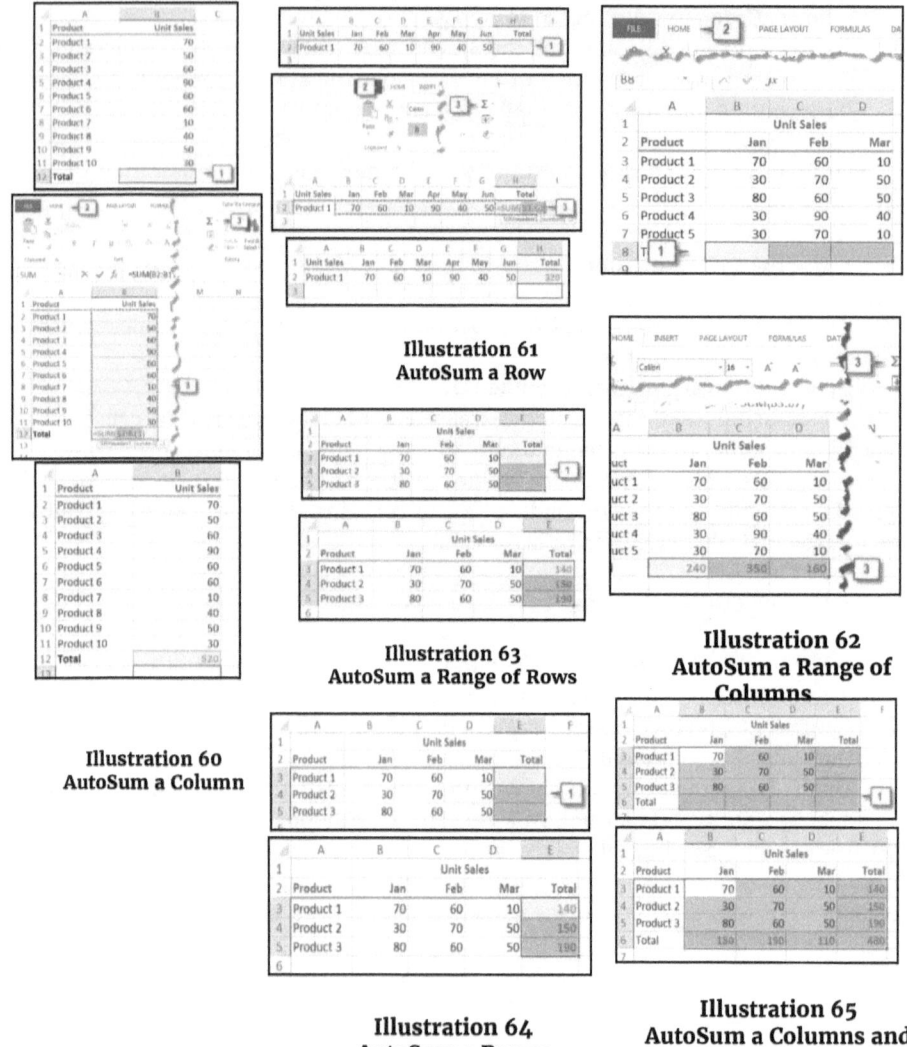

Illustration 61
AutoSum a Row

Illustration 60
AutoSum a Column

Illustration 62
AutoSum a Range of Columns

Illustration 63
AutoSum a Range of Rows

Illustration 64
AutoSum a Range

Illustration 65
AutoSum a Columns and Rows

If a cell is empty or contains a logical value, text or an error value, Spreadsheet just basically ignores the cell. If an array is not empty and contains the same, Spreadsheet will ignore the logical value, text or an error value.

When Spreadsheet evaluates arguments, if an argument is a text or logical value, Spreadsheet will be able to convert it to a umber and will be included in the count. Dates and empty arguments are also included in the count. Spreadsheet ignores the text though, if it cannot convert it to a number.

C4. Use the AVERAGE Function

The AVERAGE Function does exactly that which is calculating the average. Like the SUM and COUNT Functions discussed before, it also can include to about 255 arguments.

Syntax: AVERAGE(argument1, argument2, ...)

When the user uses this function, Spreadsheet will calculate the sum using the SUM Function and divide by the COUNT Function.

As said before, TRUE or FALSE are logical values and Spreadsheet considers numbers preceded by an apostrophe text but when using a formula or a function, Spreadsheet considers numbers enclosed in double quotes text.

When using the AVERAGE Function, as said before, how Spreadsheet treats the data type may depend on its location whether it is located in a cell, in an array or in an argument. If a cell contains a logical value, text or an error value, Spreadsheet just ignores the cell. Again, if an array contains a logical value, text or an error value, Spreadsheet ignores all three. Then if an argument contains a logical value or text, Spreadsheet includes it in the calculations.

C5. Use the MAX Function

Illustration 66
AutoSum/AutoAdd Grand Total

What the MAX Function does is that it finds the highest number and again, it could include up to 255 arguments.

Syntax: MAX(argument1, argument2, ...) where the first argument is required but the succeeding arguments are optional.

When using the MAX Function, like the previous functions, how Spreadsheet treats the data type may depend on its location whether it is located in ca cell, in an array or in an argument. If a cell contains a logical value, text or an error value, Spreadsheet just ignores the cell. If an array contains a logical value, text or an error value, Spreadsheet ignores just the text or error value.

This is because if the argument is a logical value, it is converted to its numerical value (TRUE = 1, FALSE = 0) and then it is included in the computation of the formula. Text, meanwhile returns an error because Spreadsheet is unable to convert it to a number.

As said in the previous functions, dates are stored as numbers and so the MAX Function can be used to find the latest date.

C6. Use the MIN Function

The MIN Function is the opposite of the MAX Function. Instead of searching for the highest number, the MIN Function looks for the lowest number. Again, it can include up to 255 arguments.

Syntax: MIN(argument1, argument2, ...) where the first argument is required while the succeeding or other arguments are optional.

Like in the MAX Function, dates are stores as numbers so it is possible to use the MIN Function can be used to find the earliest date.

When using the MAX Function, like the previous functions, how Spreadsheet treats the data type may depend on its location whether it is located in ca cell, in an array or in an argument. If a cell contains a logical value, text or an error value, Spreadsheet just ignores the cell. If an array contains a logical value, text or an error value, Spreadsheet ignores just the text or error value.

This is because if the argument is a logical value, it is converted to its numerical value (TRUE = 1, FALSE = 0) and then it is included in the computation of the formula. Text, meanwhile returns an error because Spreadsheet is unable to convert it to a number.

TIP: The **AutoSum Function** can be used to access most of these functions.

D. Formatting Data

Here it will be discussed how to format the data from changing the font to changing font or background colors.

D1. Change the Font

Font is the collection of character that have the same basic design and is used throughout the Office Suite. Font has been discussed before in the Word Processor lessons. To change it:
1. User must choose or highlight cells where they want to change the font.
2. Click on the Home Tab.

3. User can then click the down arrow head next to the Font box in the Font group and the gallery of fonts will open.
4. Hover the muse pointer over the list of fonts so that the Spreadsheet will provide a live view.
5. Click then the font name of the font the user requires so the Spreadsheet will apply the font to the selected cells.

NOTE: Refer to Illustration 67 in the next page.

Changing the Font of a Theme

The technical definition of 'Theme' coming from msdn.microsoft.com is the unified set of design elements and color schemes that the user can readily apply to pages of their document to give it a more consistent and attractive appearance.

To choose a font for a theme: 1.) User must choose the Page Layout Tab; 2.) User can then click Fonts in the Themes group to be able to choose the font they require from the gallery that opens.

D2. Change the Font Size

Like in Word Processor, it is also possible to change the size of the font whether the user wants to make a part of their document stand out or just wants to fit their document in a fewer pages of paper upon printing.

To proceed by use of:
- **Using the Font Size Drop Down Menu** (Refer to Illustration 68.)
  1. User must click the cell of the data whose font size they want to change.
  2. Click on the Home Tab.
  3. Click then the down arrow head next to the Font Size box in the Font group.
  4. User can then click the font size they require and the Spreadsheet will change the size of the font in the chosen cell or cells.
- **Using the Grow Font Button**
  1. User must click the cell of the data whose font size they want to change.
  2. Click on the Home Tab.
  3. User can then click the Grow Font Button in the Font group and with each click, the font size increases. Once the user has reached the size they require, they can stop clicking.
- **Using the Shrink Font Button**
  1. User must click the cell of the data whose font size they want to change.
  2. Click on the Home Tab.
  3. User can then click the Shrink Font Button in the Font group and with each click, the font size decreases. Once the user has reached the size they require, they can stop clicking.

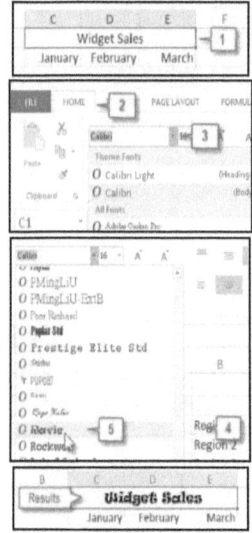

D3. Bold, Italicize or Underline

Another way of emphasizing a content on a document, besides increasing or decreasing the font, is by bolding, italicizing and slash or underlining.

It can be easily seen that the Undeline Option offer two sub-options: Underline and Double Underline. Likewise, the Format Cells dialog box offers two additional options which are: **Single Accounting** and **Double Accounting**.

Illustration 69 in the next page illustrates the difference between an Underline and a Single Accounting Underline meanwhile **Illustration 70** in the next page illustrates the difference between a Double Underline and a Double Accounting Underline.

Illustration 68
Change the Font Size

Illustration 67
Change the Font

Bold, Italicize, Underline or Single/Double Accounting Underline

1. User must select the data they want to bold, italicize, underline or single/double accounting underline.
2. Click then the Home Tab.
3. Depending on what the user requires:
   - **Bold:** After that, the user can now click the Bold Button in the Font group and the Spreadsheet will immediately bolds the data selected.
   - **Italicize:** User can now click the Italic Button and the Spreadsheet will immediately italicize the data selected.
   - **Underline or Double Underline:** User must click the down arrow head next to the Underline Button. Proceed to step 4.
   - **Single/Double Accounting Underline:** User must click the dialog box launcher in the Font group. Then they must click Format Cells and the Font Tab. Proceed to step 4.

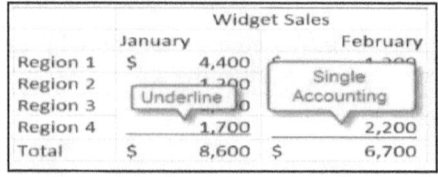

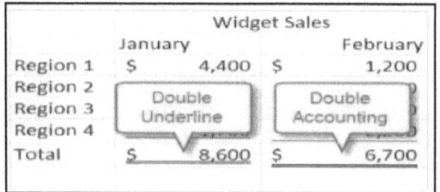

Illustration 69
Underline and Single Accounting Underline Comparison

Illustration 70
Double Underline and Double Accounting Underline Comparison

4. For:
   - **Underline or Double Underline:** User can now choose the underline they require and the Spreadsheet will apply that to the data.
   - **Single/Double Accounting Underline:** User can then click the down arrow head next to the 'Underline' field then select 'None'. Proceed to step 5.
5. For Single/Double Accounting Underline, click Ok so that the Spreadsheet underlines the data selected.

Steps illustrated in Illustrations 71 ro 73 in the next page.

NOTE: To remove the Bold, Italic or Underline, select the data or text and click on the corresponding buttons. To remove a Single/Double Accounting Undeline, click the down arrow head next to the Underline field then select None.

D4. Understanding Colors

It is possible to change the colors of data and objects in Spreadsheet. When opting to change the color of anything, Spreadsheet will present the user with the gallery of color options which has three categories:

- **Theme Colors:** These are the display set of colors that can be used for the entire document or an entire set of documents that will give it a consistent look and feel. There Is a set of colors associated with every theme and with changing the theme, the user also changes the data and objects colors. Open opening any of the application in the Office Suite, a default theme is applied.
- **Standard Colors:** These are the set of popular colors or colors used frequently. This is where when changing the theme, the data and object colors stay the same.
- **More Colors:** This option opens the 'Colors' dialog box and the user can use this to apply any color they want. When applying a color via the More Colors option, changing the theme won't affect the colors of data or objects.

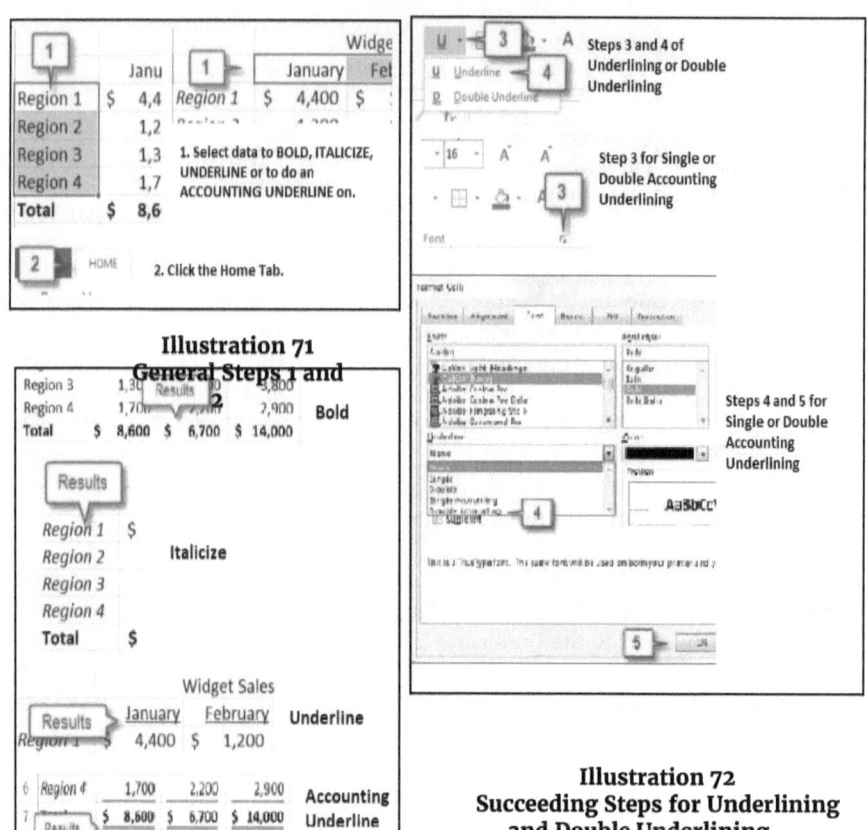

Illustration 71
General Steps 1 and 2

Illustration 72
Succeeding Steps for Underlining
and Double Underlining

Illustration 73
Results

Tabs in the Colors Dialog Box

- **Standard Tab:** User must click the Standard Tab and then the color they require.
- **Custom Tab:** User must click the Custom Tab and choose whether they require the RGB or HSL Model for their document as they are important when trying to match a color created by another program.

The RGB Model

RGB stands for Red Green Blue. This model uses the combination of the three colors to create the colors that can be displayed in the monitor. Each of the colors have a range of 0 to 255 and by adjusting the color, it is possible to produce each color of the spectrum.

The HSL Model

HSL stands for High Saturation Luminosity. Hue is a color or shade of colors; Saturation is the amount of gray in a color; And Luminosity is the amount of intensity of light found in a color. Like the RGB Model, each of these elements are assigned a range of 0 to 255 and adjusting the ranges would produce the colors of the spectrum.

Removing the Color

To remove the color of the data or object, open the Color gallery and click 'No Color'. The Spreadsheet immediately removes the color. The No Color option is not available for the Font Color Button.

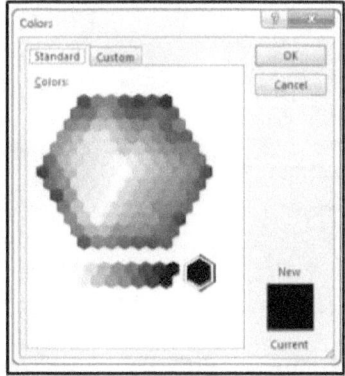 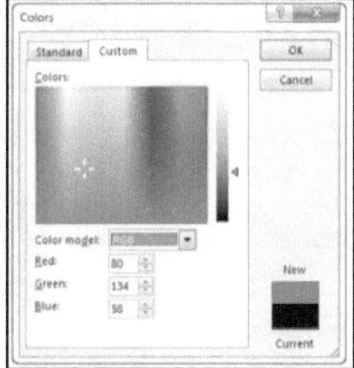

Illustration 74
Tabs in More Colors Option

D5.   Add   a   Background Color (Fill Color)

In Spreadsheet, it is possible to add background color (fill) to cells using the Fill button. To proceed:

1. User must select the cells that needed the background color.
2. Click the Home Tab.
3. User can then click the down arrow head next to the Fill button in the Font group.
4. Now, user can select the color they require or click More Colors to open the Colors dialog box to choose a color there.

To remove a background color, click the down arrow head next to the Fill button in the Font group and then click No Color. Spreadsheet instantly removes the background color.

D6. Change the Font Color

If it possible to change the background color of a cell, it is certainly possible to change the font color of a font. To proceed:

1. User must select the cells they want to change the font of.
2. Click the Home Tab.
3. User can then click on the down arrow head next to the Font Color Button in the Font group to open the color gallery.
4. Now, the user can click the color they require and Spreadsheet will make the adjustment.

To change the font color back to the default color, repeat steps 3 and 4 but instead of the user choosing the color require, they must choose 'Automatic'.

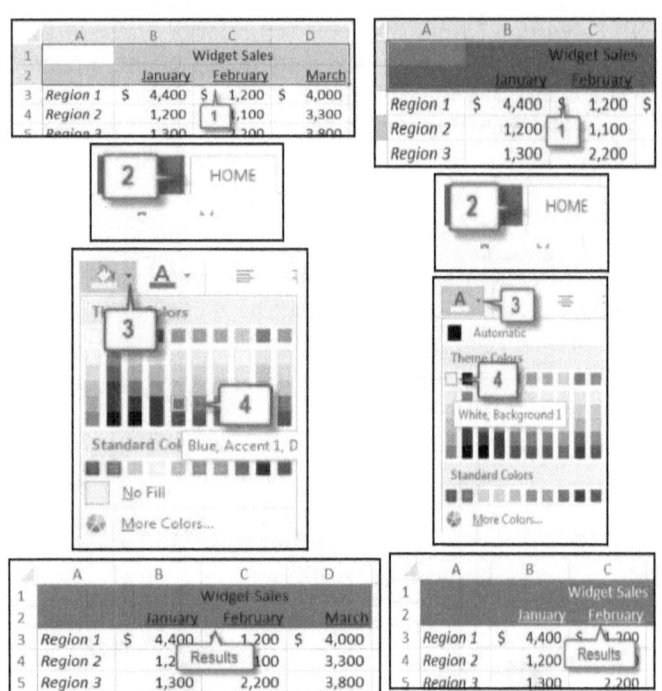

Illustration 75
Changing the Background Color

Illustration 76
Changing the Font Color

D7. Add Borders

First off, a border is a line placed to the left, right, top or bottom of a cell, a group of cells or a table.

The Borders Section of the Borders Menu

Upon clicking the down arrow head next to the Borders button, Spreadsheet will open a menu of border options. Clicking a border option from this menu will add a border line to the worksheet quickly.

- **Bottom Border** – Border will be added to the bottom of the selection.
- **Top Border** – Border will be added to the top of the selection.
- **Left Border** - Border will be added to the left side of the selection.
- **Right Border** - Border will be added to the right side of the selection.
- **No Border** – Removes the borders from all sides.
- **All Borders** - Borders will be added to the all the sides of every cell of the selection.
- **Outside Borders** - Borders will be added to the outer sides of the selected cells.
- **Thick Box Border** - Borders will be added to the outer sides of the selected cells using a thick line.
- **Bottom Double Border** – A double border will be added to the bottom of the selection.
- **Thick Bottom Border** - A thick line will be added to the bottom of the selection.
- **Top and Bottom Border** – Borders will be added to the top and bottom of the selection.
- **Top and Thick Bottom Border** – A top border and a thick bottom border will be added to the top and bottom of the selection.
- **Top and Double Bottom Border** – A top border and a double bottom border will be added to the top and bottom of the selection.

Use the Borders Section of the Borders Menu to Add a Border

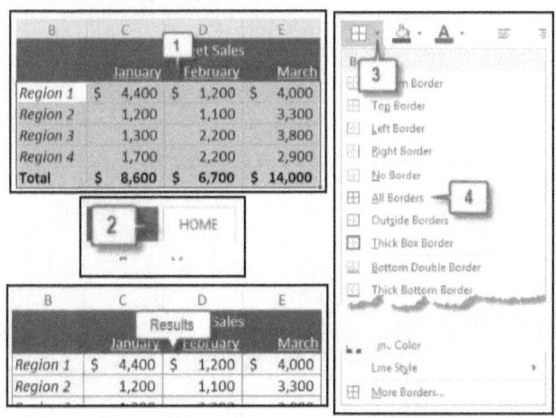

1. Select the cells that would be needing the borders.
2. Click the Home Tab.
3. User can now click the down arrow head next to the Borders button to open the menu.
4. User must now click the border they require and Spreadsheet will add said border to the selection.

Draw a Border

The five options of the 'Draw Borders' section of the 'Borders' menu are as follows:
- **Draw Border** – This turns the mouse pointer into a pencil as the user draws an outside border.
- **Draw Border Grid** – This turns the mouse pointer into a pencil with a grid as the user drags it to draw an all sides border.
- **Erase Border** – This turns the mouse pointer into an eraser that removes borders.
- **Line Color** – This opens the color menu and turns the mouse pointer into a pencil. Select the color required on the menu and use the mouse pointer to draw the border.
- **Line Style** – This opens the 'Line Style' Menu and turns the mouse pointer into a pencil. Select the line style on the menu the user required on the menu and use the mouse pointer to draw the said border.

Illustration 77
Using the Borders Section of the Borders Menu to Add a Border

To apply either one of the options, all the user has to do is to click the cell edge to place the border on said edge.

To Proceed (Refer to Illustration 78 in the next page.):
1. Choose the down arrow head next to the Borders button.
2. User can then click the 'Drawing' Option. The mouse would then turn into a pencil.
3. Click and drag the mouse pointer to draw a border.

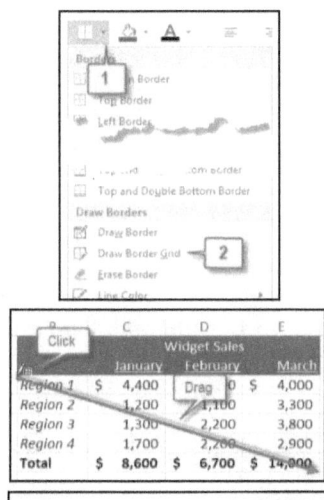

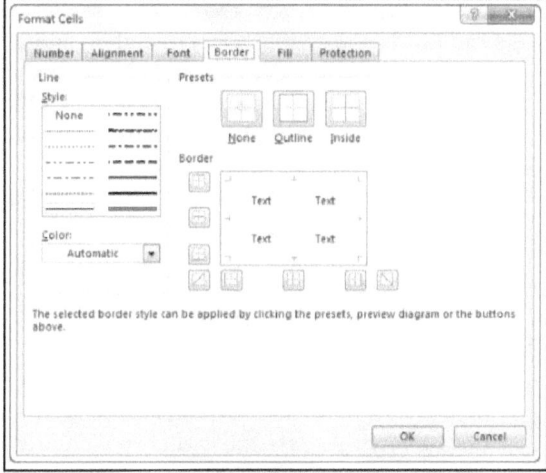

Illustration 79
Border Tab in Format Cells

Illustration 78
Draw a Border

The Border Tab in the Format Cells Dialog Box

When clicking the down arrow head next to the Borders Button and then click 'More Borders' Spreadsheet will open up the Format Cells dialog box with the Border Tab selected. The user can use the Border Tab to style the borders any way they want. Options on the Border Tab are the following:
- **Style:** User can use the Style Box so that they can choose a Line Style.
- **Color:** User can use the Style Box so that they can choose a Border Color. For application, click the down arrow head next to the Color field and then the user can choose the color they want.
- **Presets:** Preset Area contains several toggle buttons. Clicking a button in this area either applies or removes a border.
  o **None:** Click this to all the borders from the selected cells.

- o **Outline:** User must choose the style and color and then click the Outline Button to be able to place a border on the top, bottom, left and right sides of the selected cells.
- o **Inside:** User must choose the style and color and then click the Inside Button to place a border on the top, bottom, left and right sides of the selected cells but no border on the top, bottom, left and right sides that outline the user's selection.
- **Border:** Like the Presets, the Border Area also contains several buttons.
  - o **Top Border:** User must choose a style and color then they could click the Top Border Button to place a border on the top edge of the selected cells.
  - o **Inside Horizontal:** User must choose a style and color then they could click the Horizontal Border Button to place a horizontal border between each of the selected cells.
  - o **Bottom Border:** User must choose a style and color then they could click the Bottom Border Button to place a border on the bottom edge of the selected cells.
  - o **Diagonal Up Border:** User must choose a style and color then they could click the Diagonal Up Button to place a line that goes from the bottom left corner to the top right corner of the selected cells.
  - o **Left Border:** User must choose a style and color then they could click the Left Border Button to place a border on the left edge of the selected cells.
  - o **Inside Vertical:** User must choose a style and color then they could click the Inside Vertical Border Button to place a vertical border between each of the selected cells.
  - o **Right Border:** User must choose a style and color then they could click the Right Border Button to place a border on the right edge of the selected cells.
  - o **Diagonal Down Border:** User must choose a style and color then they could click the Diagonal Down Border Button to place a line that goes from the top left corner to the bottom right corner of the selected cells.

It is also possible to apply a border by clicking the graphic at the center of the Border area. First choose the style and color then click the part of the graphic where the user would want the border. Refer to Illustration 80 on the next page.

Use the Border Tab in the Format Cells Dialog Box

This (Refer to Illustration 81 on the next page.):
1. User must select the cells that need the adjustment.
2. Click the Home Tab.
3. Click then the down arrow head next to the Borders Button in the Font group to open the menu.
4. Click then 'More Borders' to open the Format Cells dialog box with the Border Tab selected.

Apply a Preset or Border and **Click to Add a Border**

1. User must click the line style they want.
2. Then they must click the down arrow head next to the Color field.
3. User can now click the color they want.
4. Depending on what to do:
   - **Apply a Preset or Border:** After that they can click a Preset Button or the Border Button if they want to apply a preset or a border. The Spreadsheet then makes the adjustment.
   - **Click to Add a Border:** After that they can click where they want to add a border. Repeat the process until the user has completed their borders. Proceed to step 5.
5. Click Ok so that Spreadsheet adds the borders.

NOTE: Refer to Illustrations 82 and 83 next page.

All Screenshot in this book was grab from Microsoft Office.

https://www.microsoft.com/en-us/legal/intellectualproperty/permissions

---

D8. Change the Text Direction

When typing text in English, in Spreadsheet by default, the text read from left to right and is horizontal. It is possible to adjust this:
1. User must select the text.
2. Click then the Home Tab.
3. User must click then the down arrow head next to the 'Orientation' Button in the 'Alignment' group.

4. The user can now click the option they want or require. Spreadsheet now changes the text direction according to user's preference.

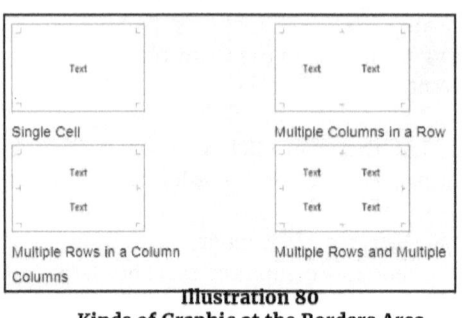

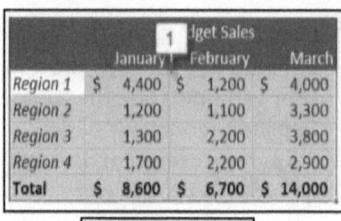

Illustration 80
Kinds of Graphic at the Borders Area

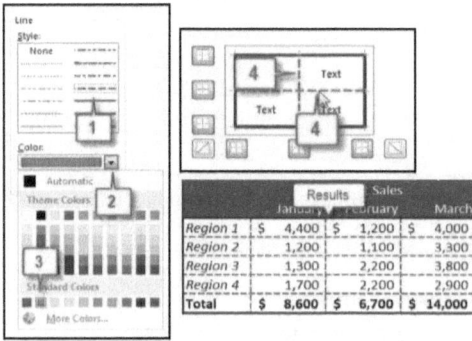

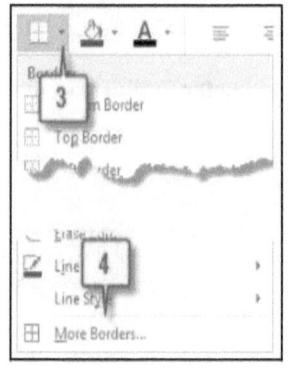

Illustration 82
Apply a Preset or Border

Illustration 81
Use the Border Tab in the Format Cells Dialog Box

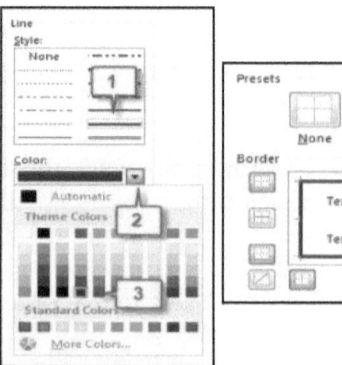

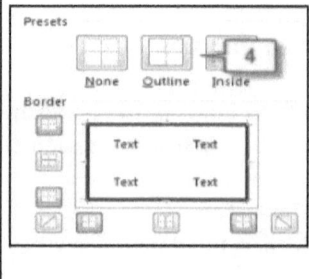

Illustration 83
Click to Add a Border

Illustration 84 illustrates the five direction options listed on the menu:

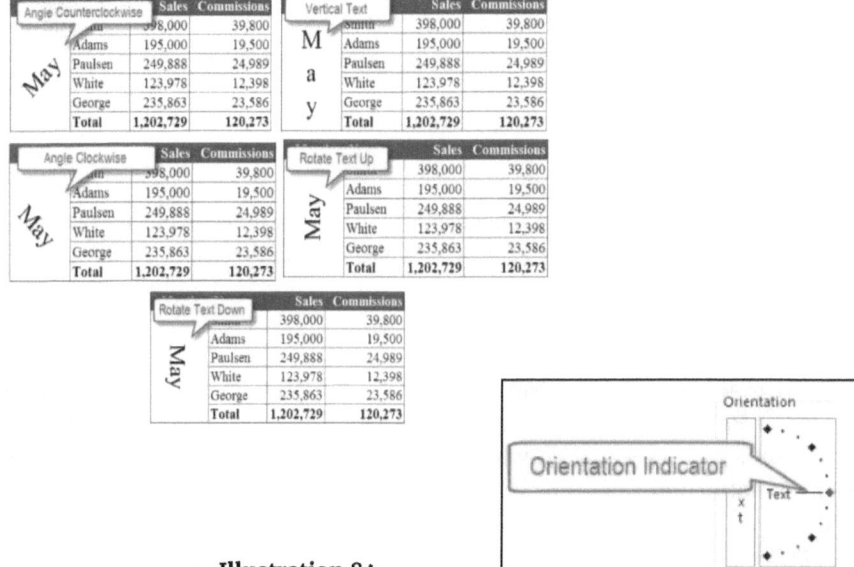

Illustration 84

Illustration 85

Manually Setting Up Text Direction

1. Select the text that needs a change in text direction.
2. User can now click the dialog box launcher in the Alignment group which opens the Format Cells Dialog Box to the Alignment Tab.
3. User must drag the orientation or they must type the number of degrees they want in the Degrees field.
4. Click Ok so that the Spreadsheet may be able to change the text orientation.

E. Conditional Formulas

Conditions are expressions or functions that produces a logical return. Conditional Formulas examine all of the conditions and determines what kind of actions to take based on the result.

E1. Using the Spreadsheet IF Function

The IF Function evaluates a condition, determines if it is TRUE or FALSE. If it is TRUE, statement returns one value. If it is FALSE, statement returns zero value.

Syntax: =IF(condition, value to return if TRUE, value to return if FALSE)

Example: User want to check if cell B1 if it is equal to 100. If it is, value to be returned must be 1000. If it is not, value to be returned is 800. The formula therefore is **=IF(B1=100,1000,800)**

NESTED IFs

If the user has more than one condition, it is still possible to use the IF Function but the user must nest it. Hence, the Nested If Function.

Example: =IF(B4=1,100,IF(B4=2,200,"Try Again"))

In the example, cell B4 is equal to 1, the condition is met so Spreadsheet will return 100. If B4 is not equal to 1, Spreadsheet will first check if it is equal to 2. If it is indeed equal to 2, Spreadsheet will return the value 200. If the value in cell B4 is not equal to both 1 and 2, Spreadsheet will return "Try Again".

NOTE: Nested Ifs are not limited to one level but can be multiple levels.

Example: =IF(B5=1,100,IF(B5=2,200,B5=3,300,"Try Again")))

In this particular example, cell B5 is checked. If it is equal to 1 and/or 2 is the same as the B4 example but if B5 is still not equal to 2, another condition will be checked. This time if B5 is not equal to 2, Spreadsheet will check of it is equal to 3. If it is , Spreadsheet will return 300 but if it still is not equal to 3, Spreadsheet will return "Try Again".

The AND Function

This function has more to do with logical expressions. It checks one or more logicals. If he logicals are **all** true, it returns TRUE. Otherwise, it returns FALSE.

Syntax: =AND(logical1, logical2, ...)

Simple Examples:
- =AND(1=1,2=2)   Result: TRUE
- =AND(1=1,2=3)   Result: FALSE

The AND function is useful when the user is working with the IF function and want to include a range of values.

A More Complex Example:
=AND(B6<100,B6>74)

In the example, if B6 is less than 100, the first logical will return TRUE. On the second expression, if B6 is greater than 74, the second logical will return TRUE. When both logical are TRUE the function will return TRUE.

An IF Example Using An AND Function (Formula used in Illustration 85.):
=IF(B7=100,1000,IF(AND(B7<100,B7>74)=TRUE,800,IF(AND(B7<75,B7>49)=TRUE,600,IF(AND(B7<50,B7>-1),400,"Invalid Entry"))))

Illustration 85
An IF Example Using An AND Function

Illustration 86
An IFS Example Using An AND Function

E2. Using the Spreadsheet IFS Function

The said function similarly works to a Nested If. It is possible to examine multiple conditions with it. Compared to a Nested If, the IFS function is simpler to use and easier to understand because one If function will not be needed to be nested within another If function.

Syntax: =IFS(condition, value to return if TRUE, condition, value to return if TRUE, condition, value to return if TRUE, ...)

Example: =IFS(B1=1,100,B1=2,200,B1=3,300)

In the example, if the value in B1 is equal to 1, Spreadsheet will return 100; If equal to 2, Spreadsheet will return 200; And if equal to 3, Spreadsheet will return 300. If the value in B1 is not equal to 1,2 or 3, Spreadsheet will return #N/A.

The AND Function

What an AND Function is has been discussed in the IF Function lesson. As said, if **all** the logicals are all true, the function returns TRUE; Otherwise, it returns FALSE.

An IFS Example Using An AND Function (Formula used in Illustration 86 in the previous page.):
=IFS(B4=100,1000,AND(B4<100,B4>74)=TRUE,800,AND(B4<75,B4>49)=TRUE,600,AND(B4<50,B4>-1),400,TRUE,"Invalid Entry")

E3. Using the Spreadsheet SUMIF Function

This function finds all of the values in the chosen range that meet the criteria the user specifies and adds them all or adds the values in a corresponding range.

Syntax: =SUMIF(range, criteria, [range to sum])

The elements:
- **Range** – This is the range of values that are needed to test the criteria against and also the range of values to sum if there is no 'Range of Sum' specified.
- **Criteria** – This is the condition that needs to be met for the value to be included in the sum.
- **Range to Sum** – This is the range of values to be summed. This is also optional.

Criteria can be a date, a time, an integer, a decimal, a logical (TRUE or FALSE), text or a logical expression. What is a logical expression? It is an expression that includes a comparison operator. Something like ">10". If a logical expression references a cell, a user must place an ampersand (&) before the cell address. It makes be considered that text and logical expressions should be enclosed in quotes and the text criteria is not case sensitive.

It is also possible to use wildcards with text criteria. An asterisk (*) matches any sequence of characters and a question mark (?) matches any single character.

Wildcard Examples:
- **Asterisk:** ABC*123 matches ABC---123 or ABC-/@4-123 or ABC+123.
- **Question Mark:** ABC?123 matches ABC-123 or ABC/123 or ABCD123. It will **not** match ABC---123 or ABC-/@4-123.

To note, if the user wants to match the asterisk or a question mark, place a tilde (~) before the character.

SUMIF Examples:

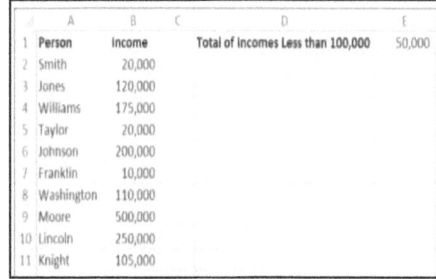

Illustration 87
Example 1

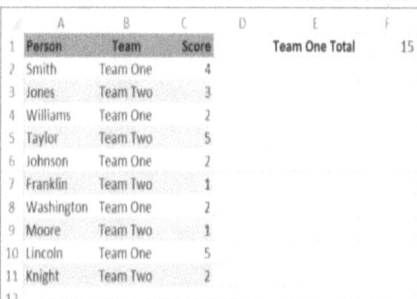

Illustration 88
Example 2

Example 1 (Illustration 87): =SUMIF(B2:B11,"<100000")

User has a list of incomes in B2 to B11 and they want to find the sum of those that are less than $100,000.

Example 2 (Illustration 88): =SUMIF(B2:B11,"Team One",C2:C11)

User has a mixed list of two teams and want to find the total score for Team One. Team names are in B2 to B11 with the scores in C2 to C11.

E4. Using the Spreadsheet AVERAGEIF Function

This function finds all the values in a range that meet the criteria the user specifies to either averages them or average the values with a corresponding range.
Syntax: =AVERAGEIF(range, criteria, [range to average])

The elements:
- **Range** – This is the range of values that are needed to test the criteria against and also the range of values to average if there is no 'Range to Average' specified.
- **Criteria** – This is the condition that needs to be met for the value to be included in the average.
- **Range to Sum** – This is the range of values to be averaged. This is also optional.

Examples:

	A	B	C	D	E
1	Person	Income		Average of Incomes Less than 100,000	20,000
2	Smith	30,000			
3	Jones	120,000			
4	Williams	175,000			
5	Taylor	20,000			
6	Johnson	200,000			
7	Franklin	10,000			
8	Washington	110,000			
9	Moore	500,000			
10	Lincoln	250,000			
11	Knight	105,000			

Illustration 89
Example 1

	A	B	C	D	E	F
1	Person	Team	Score		Team One Average	3
2	Smith	Team One	4			
3	Jones	Team Two	3			
4	Williams	Team One	2			
5	Taylor	Team Two	5			
6	Johnson	Team One	2			
7	Franklin	Team Two	1			
8	Washington	Team One	2			
9	Moore	Team Two	1			
10	Lincoln	Team One	5			
11	Knight	Team Two	2			

Illustration 90
Example 2

Example 1 (Illustration 89 on the previous page.): =AVERAGEIF(B2:B11,"<100000")

User has a list of incomes in B2 to B11 and they want to find the average of all incomes that are less than $100,000.

Example 2 (Illustration 90 on the previous page.): =AVERAGEIF(B2:B11,"Team One",C2:C11)

User has a mixed list of two teams and want to find the average score for Team One. Team names are in B2 to B11 with the scores in C2 to C11.

E5. Using the Spreadsheet COUNTIF Function

This function finds all of the values in a range that meet the criteria specified by the user and counts them.

Syntax: =COUNTIF(range, criteria)

The elements:

- **Range** – This is the range of values that are needed to test the criteria against.
- **Criteria** – This is the condition that needs to be met for the value to be included in the count.

Examples:

Illustration 91
Example 1

Illustration 92
Example 2

Example 1 (Illustration 91): =COUNTIF(B2:B11,"FEMALE")

The user has a list of people where their sex is listed on the cells B2 to B11 and they want to count the number of people who are female.

Example 2 (Illustration 92): =COUNTIF(C2:C11,">"&F1)

The user has a list of people whose ages are listed in cells C2 to C11 and they want to find the number of people whose ages are greater than the criteria in cell F1.

Chapter 5: Presentation

OBJECTIVES: This chapter will enable the user to learn about Presentation; What is it and its most basic operations.

A. The Presentation Window

Presentation is the third application in the Office Suite that is going to be discussed. In Microsoft Office, this is better known as Microsoft Excel.

Typically used by people in all fields to present lessons, plans, programs and the like with the use of slideshows that can be easily edited and saved.

In this lesson, the Presentation Window will be discussed in detail but basically, user uses this to interact with Presentation. Presentation window illustrated by Illustration 93.

A1. The Office Button

This is located at the upper left corner of the window that when clicked, opens the menu. The user will be able to use the menu to create a new file, open an existing one, save a file or perform many more other tasks.

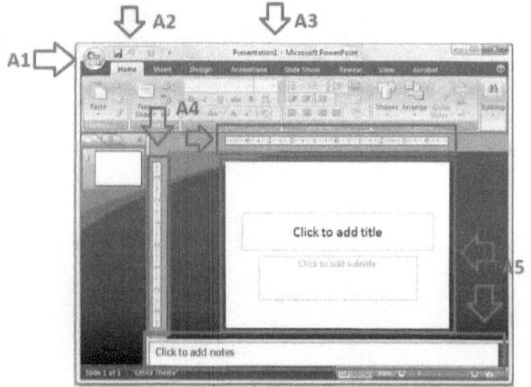

Computer Application in Entrepreneurship

A2. The Quick Access Toolbar (QAT)

Located next to the Office Button, QAT provides the user with access to the commands frequently used. Save, Undo and Redo appear on the QAT by default.

A3. The Title Bar

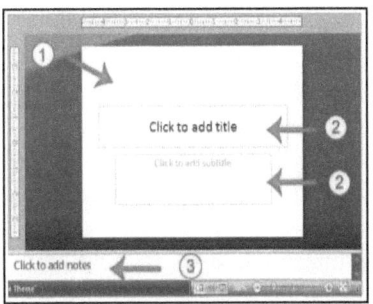

Illustration 94
Slides, Placeholders and Notes

Located at the top center of the Presentation window, this displays the name of the presentation currently being worked on. Like Word and Spreadsheets, Presentation names the presentation files sequentially but a user has the choice to change the name to their preferences.

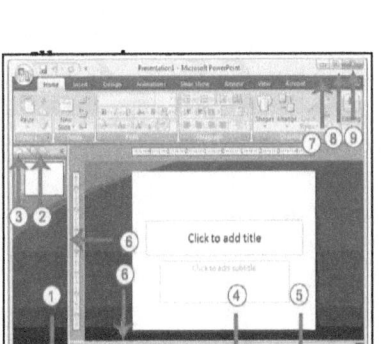

Illustration 95
Status Bar, Tabs, View Buttons and More

A4. Rulers

These are vertical and horizontal guides which the user uses to determine where they want to place an object. If these are not seen in the window, click the 'View' Tab then click 'Ruler' in the Show/Hide group. The rulers will then appear on the window.

A5. Slides, Placeholders, and Notes (Illustration 94)

1. **Slides**: These appear in the center of the window. User creates their presentations on this.
2. **Placeholders**: These holds the objects within the slides and are used to hold either text or objects such as images, clip arts and many more.
3. **Notes**: The Notes Area can be used by the user to create notes for themselves which they will be able to go back to during presenting their presentations.

A6. Status Bar, Tabs, View Buttons and More (Illustration 95)

1. **Status Bar**: Generally is located at the bottom of the window, this displays the number of the slide that is currently being edited, the total number of slides, and the name of the template in use or the name of the background.
2. **Outline Tab**: This displays the text contained in the presentation.
3. **Slides Tab**: This displays the thumbnail of all the slides which the user may be able to click to view that particular slide.
4. **View Buttons**: These appear near the bottom of the screen and can be used to change between:
   - **Normal View:** This splits the screen into three major sections: The Outline and Slides Tabs which are located on the left side of the window and enables the user to shift between two different ways of viewing the slides. The Slide Tab shows thumbnails of the slides while the Outline Tab shows the text of those slides; The Slide Pane shows the large view of the slide that the user is currently working on; And the Notes Area which appears below the Slide Pane allows the user to jot down notes for themselves.
   - **Slide Sorter View:** This shows the user the thumbnails of all their slides which they can easily delete, change the order or add new slides.
   - **Slide Show:** This is used when the user wants to view their slides as they would look in the final presentation. Commands while in this view:
     - **Esc** – Returns to the view that the user had been using previously.
     - **Left-Clicking** – Moves to the next slide or animation effect and when the last slide is reached, the user would automatically return to the previous view.
     - **Right Clicking** – This opens a pop-up menu that can be used to navigate the slides, add speaker notes, select a pointer and mark said presentation.
5. **Zoom**: This allows the user to zoom in and out on the window. Zooming in makes the window larger so that the user may be able to focus on an object while zooming out makes the window smaller so that the user may be able to see the entire window.
6. **Vertical and Horizontal Splitter Bars**: The user can click and drag on these to change the size of the panes.
7. **Minimize Button**: This is to remove the window from view but the title is visible on the taskbar.
8. **Maximize or Restore Button**: User must click the Maximize Button to cause the window to fill the screen while clicking the Restore Button returns the window to its former smaller size.
9. **Close Button**: Click this to exit the window and close the program.

B. **Creating the User's First Presentation**

The user creates the presentation on slides where the layouts are used to organize the content on each slide. Presentation has several slide layouts to choose from and like Word Processor, also has themes, with preprogrammed slide design and backgrounds, font color and effects, to choose from.

B1. Create a Title Slide

When starting the Presentation, the Presentation displays the title slide in the slide pane where the user can type the title of their presentation and the subtitle on this slide. To enter the text:
- User must click and type the title of their presentation in the area that says "Click to add title".
- User must also type a subtitle in the area that says "Click to add subtitle".

If the user does not wish to use the slide, all they have to do is click the Delete Slide Button in the Slides group in the Home Tab.

B2. Create New Slides

When the user has completed the title slide, they can now add additional slides. To proceed creating said slides:
1. First, user must click the Home Tab.
2. They can choose then the Slide Button in the Slides group which opens the Office Theme dialog box and displays several layout templates.
3. User can now click the layout they require which then appears on the slide pane of the Presentation window.
4. To add the text, all the user has to do is to click within the placeholder and type.
5. To add an additional slide in the presentation, the user had to do one of the following:
   - Right-click on the slide layout to open the menu. That's when the user can click the layout they want or require.
   - Click on the Home Tab then the Slide Button. That is when they can choose the slide layout that the user wants or requires.

B3. Make Changes to Slides

After the user creates a slide, they would want to **add text**:
1. User must place the mouse pointer at the space they would want to add text.

2. They can now type the information they want to add.

If the user would like to **change the text**:
1. User must select the text they want to change.
2. Then they can type the new text.

It is possible to use the Backspace Key to delete text. It is also possible to delete text by highlighting it and pressing the delete key.

B4. Apply a Theme

Theme is a preprogrammed set of fonts, colors and special effects that provide attractive backgrounds for the slides.

To apply a theme **on all** of the slides:
1. User must click the 'Design' Tab.
2. After which, user must choose the More Button in the Themes group.
3. This is only when the user can click the design layout they require.

To apply a theme **on some** of the slides:
1. Choose the Slides Tab which is located on the left side of the window.
2. User must hold the Ctrl Key and then click to select the slides which they would want to apply a theme.
3. They can then click the Design Tab.
4. User must then choose the More Button in the Themes group.
5. User can now right-click the theme they require to open a menu.
6. Then the user must click Apply to Selected Slides so that the Presentation may be able to apply the themes to the slides selected.

To add a dramatic effect to the theme by applying background:
1. User must choose the Design Tab.
2. Then they must click the Background Styles Button.
3. The user can now click the background they want or require.

B5. Running the Presentation Slide Show

1. Do any of the following:
   - Press F5.
   - Click on the Slide Show Tab then the From the Beginning Button in the Start Slide Show group.

- User can click the Slide Show icon in the bottom right corner of the screen.
2. This is when the slideshow appears on the computer screen.

Navigating the Slide Show

- Go to the Next Slide: Do one of the following: Press either the Right Arrow, the Enter, the Page Down Keys or Left Click the slide.
- Go to the Previous Slide: Do one of the following: Press either the Left Arrow, Backspace or the Page Up Keys.
- To End the Slide Show and Go Back to Presentation: Press the Esc Key.

C. **Animations, Transitions, Spell Check, Outline Tab, Slides Tab, Sorter View and Printing**

Animations are used by the user to control how objects move onto, off of and around the slides. Transitions are used by the user to control how the presentation moves from one slide to the next.

C1. Add Animations

It is possible to animate objects on the user's slides. There are four types of Presentation animations:
1. **Entrance:** This determines the manner to which an object appears on the slide.
2. **Emphasis:** This does something to draw attention to an object.
3. **Exit:** This determines the manner an object leaves a slide.
4. **Motion Paths:** This determines how an object moves around the slide.

After adding an animation, the user can use the Custom Animation pane to modify said animation by choosing an effect from the pane.

If the 'Auto Preview' box on the Custom Animation pane is checked, Presentation will provide the user with the preview of the animation after they have created it and each time it is modified. It is also possible to use the Play button on the Custom Animation pane for the user to able to preview it.

Choosing an effect:
1. User must select the object they want to animate.
2. They can then click the Animations Tab.
3. Click then the Custom Animations Button so that the Custom Animation pane will open.
4. User must then choose the Add Effect Button and a menu will open.

5. User can now choose the type of effect they would want or require. At this point, a submenu will open.
6. Finally, the user can click the effect they would want or require and the Presentation would apply the effect.

Modifying an Effect:
1. Click the down arrowhead next to the 'Start' field on the Custom Animations pane for the user to be able to select the start method they would require.
2. Click the down arrowhead next to the 'Property' field on the Custom Animations pane for the user to be able to select the property they would require. Property field can be labeled Direction, Size or another.
3. Click the down arrowhead next to the 'Speed' field on the Custom Animations pane for the user to be able to select the speed at which their animation must be applied.

To Preview the animation created, user must click the Play Button on the Customs Animations pane.

C2. Add Transitions

Transitions determine how the user's presentation moves from one slide to the next which can offer when the presenter clicks the mouse or after the amount of time the user specified. Presentation provides several methods of transitions.

Apply a transition to selected slides:
1. Located on the Slides Tab, the user must hold down the Ctrl Key and then they should click the slides where they would want to apply the transition.
2. Click the Animations Tab.
3. Choose then the More Button in the 'Transition to this Slide' group where a menu of transitions would open.
4. The user must then choose the transition they would want or require the Presentation to apply it. As the user would roll the pointer over each transition, Presentation will provide them with a live preview.

Apply a transition to all slides:
1. Click the Animations Tab.
2. The user must then click the More Button in the Transition to this Slide group to be able to open the menu of transitions.

3. The user must then click the transition they would want to apply, and as they roll the mouse pointer over each transition, the Presentation would provide a live preview of each transition.
4. Finally, the user can now click the 'Apply to All' Button in the transition to this Slide group.

To apply sounds to transitions:
1. The user must choose the Animations Tab.
2. Click the down arrowhead next to the 'Transition Sound' field, and then the user would be able to choose the sound they would want, and as they roll the mouse pointer over each of the sounds, the Presentation would play the sound.

To set the speed of the transition:
1. The user must choose the Animations Tab.
2. Click the down arrowhead next to the 'Transition Speed' field and only then could the user choose the speed they want.

C3. Spell Check

It would be possible for Presentation check the user or presenters spelling as they type and it would display the errors with a red wavy line under the misspelled word. To correct the misspelled word, the user must right click it and choose from the list of offers from the menu that opened or select spelling to open its dialog box. If the user needs it, they can initiate a spell check anytime they want. To initiate the spell check, do one of the following:
- Press F7 on the keyboard.
- The user must choose the Review Tab then click the Spelling Button.

If the spell check did find an impossible error, the Spelling dialog box would open with the spelling error highlighted. It is okay to respond in several ways:

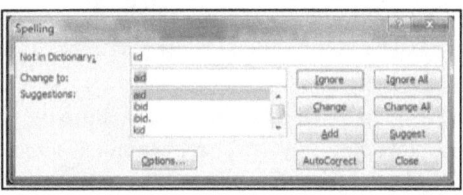

- **Do not change the spelling.** – Just click Ignore.
- **Correct Spelling.** – 1.) The user must click the correct spelling in the Suggestions box; 2.) Then click 'Change.'
- **Add to dictionary.** – Just click Add.
- **Word is correct. Do not change the presentation.** – Just click Ignore All.

Illustration 96
Spelling Dialog Box

- **Word is incorrect. Do not change the entire presentation.** – Just click Change All.

C4. Use the Outline and Slides Tab

These are located on the left side of the Presentation Window by default. The Outline Tab displays the text contained in the user's presentation while the Slides Tab displays the thumbnail of all the user's slides. To view the slide in the Slide pane, the user must click its corresponding thumbnail.

C5. Use Slide Sorter View

After the user has created their Presentation slides, the user can now move, cut, copy, paste, duplicate, navigate and view these slides in Sorter view. To view said slides in the Sorter view, do one of the following:
- Click the View Tab. After that, the user can click the Slide Sorter Button in the Presentation Views group.
- Choose the Slide Sorter Button in the bottom right corner of the Presentation Window.

Slide Sorter View Tasks and Their Corresponding Procedures

- **Move to the first slide.** – Use Ctrl+Home.
- **Move to the last slide.** – Use Ctrl+End.
- **Move to the next slide.** – Use the right arrow.
- **Move to the previous slide.** – Use the left arrow.
- **Select a slide.** – Single click the slide.
- **Open the slide in Normal View.** – Double click the slide.
- **Select slides.** – Select a single slide: User must click the slide they want to select; Select multiple slides: 1.) The user must hold down the Ctrl Key. 2.) They can now click the slides they want to select.
- **Delete a slide.** – Two Methods: 1.) a.) The user must select the slide or slides they want to delete. b.) Press the Delete Key. 2.) a.) The user must select the slide or slides they want to delete. b.) User must choose the Home Tab and then click the Delete Button.
- **Copy a Slide.** – Two Methods: 1.) a.) The user must select the slide. b.) User must click the Home Tab. c.) User can now click the Copy Button on the 'Clipboard' group. 2.) a.) The user must select the slide. b.) Press Ctrl+C.

- **Paste a slide.** - Two Methods: 1.) a.) The user must select the slide after which they would want the new slide or slides to appear. b.) User must click the Home Tab. c.) User can now click the Paste Button on the Clipboard group. 2.) a.) The user must select the slide after which they would want the new slide or slides to appear. b.) Press Ctrl+V.
- **Cut a Slide.** - Two Methods: 1.) a.) The user must select the slide or slides they want to cut. b.) User must click the Home Tab. c.) They can now click the Cut Button in the Clipboard group. 2.) a.) The user must select the slide or slides they want to cut. b.) Press Ctrl+X.
- **Move a slide.** – 1.) The user must select the slide or slides they want to move. b.) Drag chosen slide or slides to the new location.
- **Duplicate a slide.** - 1.) The user must select the slide or slides they want to duplicate. 2.) Press Ctrl+D.

C6. Print

The presentation provides the user with many printing options: They can print a large view of their slides or print them as handouts with a couple of slides per page. It is also possible to print Notes Pages or the Outline View of the user's slides.

To proceed:
1. Click the Office Button so that a menu opens.
2. The user must now choose Print.
3. Choose the Print Preview.
4. Click the down arrow head next to the 'Print What' field in the Page Setup group and only then could the user select what they would like to print. The preview appears on the screen.
5. The user then must click print which opens the Print dialog box.
6. Click then the down arrow head next to the 'Color/Grayscale' field to be able to select whether they would want their slides to print in color, grayscale or black and white. If the printer being used can only print black and white, it is only logical to choose this option.
7. Finally, click 'Ok.'

www.ingramcontent.com/pod-product-compliance
Lightning Source LLC
Chambersburg PA
CBHW020444220526
45464CB00002B/851